SUPER BASIC
LEADERSHIP

A Guide to Understanding and Developing Leadership Skills

by

PAUL D. PANTERA

Contributions by: Victor J.
Edited by: Jesse Lyn
Graphic Design by: Ravi Ramgati

Panterax Ltd

ISBN: Paperback- 978-1-957442-21-1
ISBN: Hardcover- 978-1-957442-22-8
ISBN: eBook-   978-1-957442-23-5

Dedication

This book is dedicated to any and everyone who wants to begin the journey of leadership yet doesn't know where to start. Start here, get a little better every day, enjoy the small wins, forgive the losses, embrace the lessons... be the leader.

Gratitude

I want to express my heartfelt thanks to the team that helped make this book possible: Victor J., Jesse Lyn, and Ravi Ramgati. Thank you for your time and talent in bringing this project to life.

PANTERAX

Sign up for our newsletter and
receive a FREE ebook of puzzles at:

http://pantheria.net

Table of Contents

Introduction

There are two types of people in the world, and this isn't an oversimplification because anyone who is anyone can find themselves in these two classifications. There are people who accept things as they are and are content with their place in the world. But then there are people who see a world in need of great change. They see a world that shouldn't be the way it is, a world that can be better, a world that needs the creative ideas of someone with ambition, courage, and remarkable ability to usher in a new age. Winston Churchill, Mahatma Gandhi, Nelson Mandela, Muhammad Ali, Michael Jordan, and Steve Jobs—the world they left behind in their wake was not the same as the one they entered.

At this point, you will be asking yourself if you are that kind of person. The answer isn't a no-brainer—you know you are. It doesn't matter that the names of the titans above seem like a far cry to you right now. The fact is that, like those people, your will to act and desire to see a better world needs to be greater than the challenges you need to overcome. Yes, there will be challenges that will push you towards exceptionalism. Challenges that no ordinary person can even think of carrying out. But you are not ordinary. All you need are the right tools, skills, knowledge, resources, goals, and vision to bring about a landmark transformation for the better; one that will put your name and face firmly in the hearts and minds of everyone around you as the one who accomplished it all.

But before you do, it is important to remember that no matter how lofty your goals are and how driven you are to achieve them, you cannot do it alone. Yes, you will be the main driver, but your efforts will need like-minded people who also believe in your vision and desire to bring about change. The only question is why they should believe in you. Are you the right face of the cause? Are you the one who, more than any of them, has visualized what the new world will look like? Do you have the knowledge, skills, ideas, and plans to make that vision a reality? Above all else, are you able to motivate, inspire, and lead these like-minded people into that new world?

Super Basic Leadership — A Guide to Understanding and Developing Leadership Skills is an introduction to the principles of leadership roles, types of authority, and ways to develop mature, productive relationships between leaders and their people. It is an essential guide for people ages 16 and up who have always thought of themselves as a "person of the people," whether in business, social causes, politics, and more. Young people from all walks of life who are ambitious, driven, creative, and looking to bring about a huge change in society can gain deep insights into their potential as a leader — at home, in their community, and in the world at large.

The book outlines the fundamental principles of leadership and delves into the various types of leadership across history and society. At the same time, it also thoroughly differentiates between leadership and authority, looking at the various kinds of authority exercised to achieve different goals and how they affect the people under them. This book provides new and budding leaders with insights and knowledge of how to apply leadership skills in multiple settings from an early age so that they are able to hone the much-needed skills that will enable them to influence others toward their vision. Whether it revolves around family, friends, work, community, or the global stage, being a good leader means having the right tools to help or influence others and make a positive impact.

Paul D. Pantera is a Baltimore-born Oceanside, CA resident, the CEO of Panterax Ltd, and the creator of the Pantheria Media Collection. A graduate of Clark Atlanta University and active duty Petty Officer First Class in the Navy, Mr. Pantera is an authority when it comes to leadership. His experience with young, old, amateur, or seasoned individuals aspiring to become better at their roles in life led to the creation of the Pantheria Project, which aims to instill the key qualities of self-awareness, discipline, communication, and a united knowledge, empathy approach to drive them towards success and growth.

This project was inspired by working with young service members in high-stress work environments where personal technology isn't always allowed for security and practical reasons. As part of the Pantheria Project, Mr. Pantera is also the author of *Lateral Thinking Lessons and Puzzles to Unlock Creativity and Leadership Ability: Simple and Easy Methods to Boost Brain Power in Ages 16 and Up, Pantheria Grand Book of 200 Grid Logic, Sudoku, Codeword, & Word Search Puzzles for*

Adults: A Mega-Collection of Grid Logic, Sudoku, Codewords and Wordsearches! and *The Pantheria Life Log,* a simple yet flexible journal that helps the user evaluate their current life, set goals, then write down daily meetings, tasks, and has room for notes and thoughts essential for developing discipline as a leader. In his free time, he plays video games and hosts regular cookouts for his friends and family.

Anyone can be a good leader or hold positions of authority. But effective and successful people have honed specific skills that enable them to influence others. With this book, you are going to take your very first step in understanding the kind of leader you want to be and the change you want to bring to the world.

LEADERSHIP
101

Our chief want is someone who will inspire us to be what we know we could be. –Ralph Waldo Emerson

Is leadership the same thing as being in charge? That is probably what you have seen all your life, whether it is your parents, school principal, kindergarten teacher, high school gym teacher, baseball coach, first supervisor or manager, or what-have-you. They are responsible for a group of people and determining their goals, tasks, and potential growth. But the question remains, is it the same thing as leadership? Can you honestly say that your first supervisor inspired you to take control of your life, or did they simply tell you to do the job that was given to you?

Leaders are everywhere around us, whether it is in high-end positions such as business, government, politics, education, healthcare, and religion or at the grassroots level within our own communities such as social activism, charity, community welfare programs, neighborhood watch, co-op boards, and many more. In any of these cases, the people involved all gravitate towards a single person or a group of people who have confidence, can communicate clearly and effectively, enjoy solving problems with out-of-the-box solutions, understand the importance of delegation, are ready to take calculated risks, exercise patience and clear-headedness, and aren't afraid to rock the boat when it comes to trying something new and revolutionary.

Not only do they set the tone by utilizing these skills and abilities, but they also inspire other people around them to become invested in ensuring success across the board.

Are you a leader? Do you think you know what leadership means to you? That is what we will review in this first chapter and understand where leadership begins, how it is refined, and why it is important.

Leadership Defined

The Merriam-Webster dictionary (n.d.) defines leadership as "the office or position of a leader," the "capacity to lead," and "the act or an instance of leading." The word "leader" itself is defined as "a person who leads: such as a person who directs a military force or unit, and a person who has commanding authority or influence." A person can either naturally gravitate towards the position of leader or gain such a position through a wealth of experience, talent, and skill; following which they become proficient at being decisive in difficult situations, pursuing a clear vision and plan after setting the required goals, and influencing not just the followers within their groups and teams but also the people associated with the organization's interests, such as clients, partners, rivals, and so on.

In essence, a leader is someone whose goals, vision, and influence are clearly articulated in such a way that the followers and the organization will be determined and ready to make these goals a success and the vision a reality. The leaders' influence can either be from the front lines or remain invisible and lets the organization take the necessary steps to fulfill those goals.

People have witnessed what leaders are supposed to be from a very early age. In school, teachers appear to be the most visible authority figures who encourage and motivate children for their personal development and growth. In groups of friends or clubs, pals, tribes, gangs, squads, or what-have-you, one of them strikes out as noticeably different as they affect the group because of their personality, determination, clear-headedness, ideas, and charisma. Competitive sports offer another public view of how leaders on teams use their abilities to influence the motivation of their teammates as well as devise strategies and identify each team member's strengths and weaknesses to achieve victory, especially in difficult situations.

Leadership vs. Management

There is a common misconception that leadership and management are inherently the same. This stems from some roles, such as team leaders, that are essentially middle-level management positions, so they are considered leadership roles. The reality, however, is that while leaders are more than capable of being effective managers, the same cannot be said for managers themselves. Line managers are responsible for managing the day-to-day operations of different teams within an organization. They follow the main overarching vision of the organization's leaders. Managers may be called upon to be the direct representatives of the senior leadership and motivate and inspire employees and will do so based on being inspired by the leadership and their vision.

Leaders who have advanced from junior to senior positions in the hierarchy would have done so after showing exceptional management skills and achieving goals. During that time, through learning on the field, tackling difficult situations and crises, and being mentored by inspiring leaders, they will have created their own unique leadership style and won the trust and loyalty of their teams so well that their elevation to senior leadership positions would be more than obvious. Such leaders have more of an edge over leaders who, while naturally suited to the role, have not gone through the same process of understanding the organization from top to bottom. Their primary focus is the vision they have set for the organization and leaving the day-to-day operations that lead to its achievement to the managers, supervisors, team leads, and so on.

Most family business owners, for example, make it a point to put their grown children through the lower rungs of the business so that they can see how it functions. Restaurant owners might have their kids working in the kitchens or waiting tables once they get to high school, or owners of bike messaging services have had their kids deliver messages and couriers across town. The goal here is for family business owners to instill the requisite leadership and management capabilities within their offspring so that, when the time comes, the business will be in good hands. Not only that, but the employees will also recognize that the successor is someone who has been trained and equipped for the role. The earliest known example is the "great man" theory. Though the concept of the great man theory has existed for far too long in the history of mankind, the theory itself was first presented in the 1800s by Thomas Carlyle, a Scottish historian, and philosopher.

Based on this theory, Carlyle emphasized that leaders are naturally born and gifted with the qualities of leadership and used the examples of great heroes and rulers of old such as Julius Caesar, Augustus, Alexander the Great, Genghis Khan, George Washington, Akbar, Saladin, and many others. Such leaders showed a great sense of purpose and were highly self-motivated to make their vision a reality without getting the opportunities to develop their leadership skills. Instead, they showed more mental prowess, resilience, charisma, and desire to take on the mantle of leadership and win the hearts of their followers.

In more corporate businesses, on the other hand, managers are elevated based on their performance, talents, personal qualities, confidence, and even leadership skills to climb up the ladder within the organization till they reach senior leadership positions such as the C-suite (Chief Executive Officer, Chief Finance Officer, Chief Operations Officer, Chief Technology Officer, and so on), directorships, and Vice Presidencies.

Theories Behind Leadership

Like various leadership roles, several different leaders have shown a drive for conquest and warfare but also politicians, diplomats, and activists such as Abraham Lincoln, Winston Churchill, Mahatma Gandhi, Bishop Desmond Tutu, Reverend Al Sharpton, and also business pioneers, including

John D. Rockefeller, Richard Branson, Bill Gates, Steve Jobs, Bill Gates, Tony Robbins, and so on. One of the most redeeming features of the great man leaders is an unflinching and diehard support base, full of people who have total faith in the leader's opinion, approach, ideas, and philosophy. This can lead to fanatical devotion, such as in the case of Adolf Hitler and Joseph Stalin.

The second most prominent theory behind leadership is the trait theory. Originating from the mid-20th century, the trait theory is very similar to the great man theory. The only difference is that while the great man theory suggests that leadership abilities are imbued within a leader, the trait theory argues that such abilities can be acquired through hard work, determination, practice, and experience. This theory builds upon the idea of the great man theory, that leadership is a divine right of a select few or elite by opening it up to anyone who puts their mind to it.

In contrast to the great man theory, the behavioral theory implies that people can be groomed into leadership roles. According to this theory, people can become great leaders once they are provided with the right skills, knowledge, and resources, as well as behavioral traits. For this, potential leaders observe mentors, ask questions, use trial-and-error, and improve their decision-making skills and actions with the aid of highly successful people with a proven track record in leadership.

Two other theories, called the situational and contingency theories, are also similar, with one key difference. Developed by scientist Fred Fielder in the 1960s, the contingency theory focuses on how effective and well-prepared a leader is based on the variety of situations they face, as well as the relationship of the leader with the followers. The thinking behind this is that the leadership style needs to fit with the right situation. Fielder's model highlights that a higher level of confidence and trust between the leader and follower results in a productive relationship. This can then ensure higher levels of productivity, clearer communication, and better commitment to the overall vision.

Situational theory, on the other hand, differs from contingency theory by suggesting that the situations dictate how a leader will respond rather than a leader being prepared for all situations. In situational leadership, as developed by

Dr. Paul Hersey and Kenneth Blanchard, a leader needs to show greater flexibility and adapt to the situation and how they need to lead their followers. Instead of having a matching leadership style to the situation, leaders should adapt their style to match the situation that arises. Furthermore, while the contingency theory stresses that the leader-follower relationship has a greater bearing on whether or not the leader gives priority to relationships or tasks, the complexity of the situation does the same in the situational theory.

Styles of Leadership

The various leadership theories then give birth to different leadership styles that correspond with a leader's nature, behavioral traits, thought processes, and experience. Based on these personal qualities, leaders can strategize, plan, and adapt to the needs of the business and the market. With their specific leadership style, they inspire and motivate their followers or employees to perform their tasks and achieve the organization's goals. At the same time, they consider the welfare of their followers and the expectations of their clients and partners.

Leaders should have enough understanding of their relevant style to see how well they influence their followers and employees and how they can achieve their desired results. It takes a while before leaders recognize their own particular styles; however, they may not strictly stick to one style. Usually, leaders display various traits of other styles as well, which may all come together to make their particular style. Nevertheless, their behaviors, mindsets, attitudes, personalities, and experiences make them lean towards a singular style that sets the tone for the kind of leadership that they will exhibit.

One such leadership style is the transformational leadership style which focuses more on change and transformation within different aspects such as the organization, followers, employees, approaches, methods, processes, product lines, and so on. A leader with a transformational style looks to develop better relationships between themselves and their followers and inspire them to dig deep and discover their true potential. This may involve taking their followers from their existing state and transforming them into something better through trial and error, training, and mentoring so that the followers can become different and improved versions of themselves. Such a leadership style is particularly helpful for organizations that are constantly evolving or looking to evolve or make dramatic changes in order to keep up with the rest of the world.

Ideally, a leader with a transformational approach is looking to find more ways in which their organizations and followers can evolve, change, and become better than they already are. They will look towards developments that may take place in the future and be ready to adapt the organization and followers to be better suited for those developments when they come. At the same time, such leaders also have to make sure that these changes are something that the followers are also ready to accept and willing to incorporate within themselves.

The goal of transformational leadership is to ensure that not only is the organization itself staying up to date and ready to evolve for the next best thing but also to offer followers more growth and improvement within themselves. This growth and improvement are obvious from gaining greater proficiency in different skills and overall satisfaction in their role.

On the other hand, the authoritarian leadership style is used by leaders who prefer to keep their organizations and processes within a fixed ecosystem. In such a leadership style, the idea of change can only come from the leaders themselves, and contributions and feedback about positive changes from followers, employees, clients, partners, and so on are rarely welcomed. Instead, the leaders decide whether or not a particular change is necessary, and it may actually compromise the well-being of the followers and employees.

To take it to extreme levels, authoritarian leadership styles are mostly used by dictators or people in positions of power who prefer to have their decisions revered rather than questioned. Authoritarian leaders like things the way they are and do not need to rock the boat unless they feel there is a major opportunity for profit. In most cases, they may not be able to see any negative impact or impending disaster due to tunnel vision based on their authoritarian leadership style, and it may be too late before any changes can be implemented.

Unlike the authoritarian style, the authoritative leadership model involves mentoring followers rather than commanding them toward a particular goal. Instead of making it mandatory for followers to stick to the course charted by a leader, the authoritative leadership style focuses on inspiring employees to follow leaders toward a common goal and fulfilling a shared vision. In such a leadership style, feedback is shared from leader to follower and vice versa. This means that the lines of communication are kept open, and ideas are bounced around so that everyone is properly aligned with the vision.

Moreover, the authoritative leadership style also helps leaders get to know their followers better, particularly on a more personal level. They become invested in the success of their followers and offer them more insights, mentorship, guidelines, tools, and resources to succeed on their path toward achieving the organization's goals and vision.

This leadership style is ideal for helping followers towards their personal growth, which in turn contributes to the organization's vision. However, leaders have to be careful not to become too heavily invested in their followers, especially in their day-to-day activities. Doing so can result in becoming more hands-on with their followers and the routine tasks instead of letting them act of their own volition. Followers may feel that they are being micromanaged rather than inspired or motivated, which can cause friction between not just the followers and the leader, but among the followers themselves.

Instead, an approach that focuses on delegation is considered more productive, hence the delegative leadership style, also known as "laissez-faire." While an authoritative leadership style may seem more hands-on and involved, the delegative leadership style empowers the followers and makes them feel more trusted and valued as team members. Leaders can delegate tasks and responsibilities to their followers with total confidence from knowing that they are highly suited for the job and can navigate any tricky situations deftly. This style also allows followers to gain more confidence in their abilities, flex their creative muscles, seek out-of-the-box solutions, and ultimately grow as professionals, thus making them appreciate their leaders and mentors even more.

For the delegative leadership style to succeed, however, a leader must be completely confident in the abilities and talents of their followers. Leaders should keep a close eye on their team's activities while not getting too hands-on, but they must also be ready to offer constructive feedback and criticism as and when needed. There will be times when followers, no matter how resourceful or talented, are faced with a problem they cannot overcome. For this, leaders have to create an environment where their followers can come to them in times of trouble without the fear of harsh criticism or reprisals.

Other styles, such as the participative leadership style, make leaders more receptive to the feedback of their followers and employees. In the participative style, leaders appreciate the suggestions and involvement of the followers as they also have certain expertise about how goals should be achieved. Doing so makes the organization more open, inclusive, and collaborative and makes the followers feel a greater share of the responsibility. They feel that they have more of a say in the organization's vision in an environment that is more democratic, cooperative, and accountable. This environment brings together varied experiences and viewpoints to make decision-making and problem-solving a lot easier through open communication, trust-building, mutual reliance, and understanding. Everyone bears the responsibility in case something goes wrong rather than blaming individuals.

And finally, the transactional leadership style creates more of a give-and-take environment where leaders provide praise and rewards whenever followers do things right but also implement reprimands and even punishments whenever mistakes are made. Goals are set, and followers understand what rewards they are entitled to, usually bonuses, incentives, perks, giveaways, and so on. In an environment with a transactional leadership style, followers understand what roles they have and what is expected of them and that there is no room for major change or transformation, at least from their end.

Leaders expect their followers to abide by set guidelines and fulfill their goals so that they can be rewarded appropriately. All the leaders have to do is oversee the operations to ensure that everything is running smoothly, much like a managerial role. Though transactional leadership may seem beneficial to the followers for its reward system and to the leader for the fulfillment of the organization's goals, it stifles any creativity or growth within followers, and they feel like their talents are stagnating unless they contribute anything transformational to the organization.

Why Leadership Is Important

Effective and influential leadership has several important benefits, not just for the leaders themselves but also for the followers, employees, organizations, and the people directly in contact with them. Their actions and influence inspire sweeping changes across the board that help to transform the landscape of their operations and organization, not to mention their foresight and decision-making skills to see what effects the changes will induce. Through the leader's actions and directions, teams will be able to implement the changes that will benefit everyone involved and understand the overarching vision leaders have for where they want the organization to be in the future.

This will require convincing followers why the leader's vision is what is best for the organization and for them as well. Leaders need to make their followers realize how their efforts, abilities, and creativity are necessary to make the vision a reality. Each follower or employee brings something unique to the table, and a leader has to see how all of their unique talents will blend together to make a fully-equipped machine ready to take on the challenges set in front of them. This also helps followers see how exactly they contribute to the end goals and what is expected of them.

This, in turn, also creates an environment of positivity, appreciation, and recognition. When leaders recognize exactly how their followers are making a difference, they do not hesitate to show their admiration, either verbally or through incentives and gestures. Not only does it make the followers feel appreciated, but it also boosts confidence in their abilities and improves morale among everyone, showing them that everyone is able to make strides and grow professionally through hard work, dedication, and creativity. This will make them more willing to come up with new ideas and methods, work harder to gain more appreciation and recognition, and bring them one step closer to their vision.

In order to do this, leaders will be more than willing to help their followers by providing the necessary resources, facilities, comforts, and motivation they need to feel at home and feel like a valued part of the organization. By listening to their followers' concerns, apprehensions, and problems, leaders can work towards putting them at ease and offering them security and reassurance, as well as keeping the environment positive, friendly, encouraging, and collaborative. Only then can leaders have their followers invested in working towards their vision and ensuring success.

It also helps leaders connect with their followers on a deeper and personal level, which makes assigning responsibilities and providing guidance easier and more transparent. Moreover, it also helps them handle conflict resolution, especially among their team members. The environment created by leaders allows followers to be open about bringing problems to their notice and confident that they will receive the best kind of consideration. For leaders, resolving conflicts is an eye-opening experience about the problems their followers face. Once they understand those problems, leaders can devise ideas and solutions that will mitigate those problems in the future.

Leadership is also an important conduit for setting an example for their followers. Showing followers how it's done, rolling up one's sleeves and getting into the thick of the tasks, being ready to inspire and clarifying any confusion create a positive image of the leader's investment in their followers and their success. Furthermore, followers are inclined towards following their leaders' example and modeling themselves according to their habits, decisions, and preferences. Like children following the examples of their parents and teachers, followers need guidance and a roadmap of how to achieve success, and the most obvious choice is to follow in their leaders' footsteps, if not be mentored by them.

There are several other reasons why leadership is very important. Leaders understand what the purpose of the organization is and how to achieve that purpose through the collective efforts of the entire team. Not only do they understand this, but they also make sure that it is communicated clearly and effectively to the team and followers so that there are no ambiguities about what the purpose is. Furthermore, they also do their best to ensure that the purpose and guidelines are being followed properly by the team and step in whenever necessary so that they can reinforce them. The same goes for promoting essential values that are important for the organization and the team's success. Values such as honesty, punctuality, trustworthiness, hard work, diligence, confidence, and so on are essential for the organization's continued growth. The leader is the best template that incorporates such values for followers to do the same.

Leaders should also inspire their followers to get their creative juices flowing. At the same time, leaders must ensure that creativity doesn't interfere with too many of the organization's set procedures and guidelines. Nevertheless, fostering creativity within a team allows the followers to make a valuable contribution to the organization and feel that they are growing personally and professionally. Once employees, followers, and team members show signs of creativity, they can then figure out ways to improve an organization's procedures, productivity, and efficiency, as well as deliver on projects a lot faster.

Communication is also an essential ingredient of successful leadership. Leaders need to be clear about the message they deliver to their team members, not to mention the instructions and guidelines. A leader's communication can be clear, concise, and elaborate with relevant, friendly, and uplifting details as they communicate the organization's policies and procedures, encourage motivation, and harbor a friendly work environment.

Clear communication also helps leaders to convey the vision of the organization that they have in their minds so that everyone is on the same page. The communication style should also be passionate about what vision leaders want the organization to achieve. That same passion will help the followers to be as driven as the leader toward achieving that vision.

Other qualities and values that are instilled thanks to effective and successful leadership include a commitment to the organization and its vision, fostering ethical values and integrity when it comes to the organization's dealings, confidence among employees while they are working, interacting with clients, partners, or management, improved morale, trust in the process, better coordination among the team members, and a sense of personal and professional growth.

2

LEADERSHIP ROLES
AND CHARACTERISTICS

*If your actions inspire others to dream more, learn more, do
more and become more, you are a leader.*
–John Quincy Adams

B y the time you are fully on your journey to becoming
the leader you deserve to be, you will take on different
character traits that are the hallmark of great leaders
everywhere, which will continue to enhance your unique style
of leadership. At the same time, you will also understand the
roadmap a lot better, which stops you have to make, what
you need to do to move on to the next level, and how you can
inspire people along the way. Whether you are an intern or a
junior associate, an executive or a manager, everything you
do and learn is helping you consolidate your understanding
of what your role as a leader will require. This experience is
going to keep adding to your knowledge about which targets

to achieve, what metrics to score, and where to focus your energy.

To understand what your roadmap to leadership must look like, you have to familiarize yourself with the various leadership roles in diverse organizations, whether they are at the grassroots level, in academics, or different sizes and types of business. It's important to know what role you ideally need to be in, a CEO, a VP, a director, and so many more, and what each of these roles entails in terms of authority, innovation, and transformation. This chapter aims to help you recognize these roles, how each leader progresses into them, and what characteristics are required to excel at them.

The Roles of Strategists and Visionaries

To start with, we have strategists who, as the name suggests, look out for the larger strategy that is in play at an organization. They possess strong analytical skills, which they will need to anticipate any problems or concerns that can stand in contrast to the organization's goals and strategy, come up with reasonable solutions, and make adjustments to their plans in order to achieve the best resolutions. Strategists are detail-oriented when it comes to creating properly sequenced plans that are aligned with the organization's goals. These plans provide everyone with the necessary guidelines for achieving these goals and what to do when a problem arises.

Strategists also take stock of the situations in front of them and must analyze whether or not to adopt a certain strategy towards them or make amendments to their strategies that are tailored to resolving those concerns. Once they evaluate the available information regarding a problem, strategists must then devise necessary solutions while also abiding by the organization's values, goals, and overarching vision. These solutions will determine the organization's priorities, particularly in terms of budget and manpower allocation, training requirements, technological enhancements, and so on.

Because strategists need to have foresight about what kind of problems to expect and how best to tackle them, they have their finger on the pulse of the business world and the marketplace to see what areas the organization needs to capitalize on. This includes looking at the movements of competitor organizations, gaining valuable feedback from clients, partners, and employees, understanding the needs of their target customers, analyzing their own strengths and weaknesses as well as those of their competitors, and identifying areas of improvement and innovation. Once strategists have all this information available, they can chart out the strategies that will help the organization meet the challenges set by a dynamic market landscape and demanding clientele, as well as strive for growth as a market leader. Their strategies will create a lasting impression in the minds of clients and partners, as these strategies offer organizations a competitive edge.

At the same time, strategists must also resort to careful maneuvering of the organization's stakeholders, such as the top leadership and department heads. They familiarize themselves with the priorities of the different power players, such as directors, senior executives, department heads, and the like, in order to understand their motivations and how they perceive the organization's vision. Strategists can then advise, lobby, and steer the relevant stakeholders toward the bigger picture. They can also act as mentors to their own team members by looking out for their interests, identifying their talents, and channeling their abilities toward the grand vision that they have foreseen.

Oftentimes, employees believe that by following existing procedures and practices, they can keep their performance levels at acceptable levels. This stifles creativity which subdues their passion, energy, talents, and confidence, ultimately leading to stagnation when it comes to innovating. This is where strategists recognize the signs and work their magic to unlock their employees' suppressed creativity by providing them with opportunities and roles that place them firmly in the big picture.

Strategists have various roles and titles within an organization. They work at the highest levels of the hierarchy, such as a board of directors, chief executive officers, entrepreneurs, Strategic Business Unit (SBU) executives, and senior managers. The board of directors usually consists of shareholders and, depending on the organizational structure, can be at the very top of the hierarchy or under the top individual. The board is in charge of major decision-making, particularly when the top leader is unable to discharge those duties or is incapacitated.

The board of directors has a broad agenda, such as the operational management of an organization, development of new products and services, collaboration with partners, incorporation of new technology, appointment and evaluation of senior executives, goal-setting, and financial management, among other things. They ensure that the relevant stakeholders stay aligned with the organizational principles, procedures, and values. Aside from business organizations, the board of directors can take different names and titles, such as councils, elders, joint chiefs, etc.

Aside from the board of directors, strategists can also take the form of a CEO or a president, as well as entrepreneurs and SBU-level executives. Again, this individual can be above or below the board of directors. A CEO's main focus is keeping the organization successful and viable, as well as steering the organization's focus and resources on a particular set of priorities that they give the most importance to at any given time. As CEOs are strategists, they also see the big picture and factor in all the avenues that could directly impact the organization's vision.

CEOs, as well as others in the C-suite such as CFOs, CTOs, COOs, and the like, will have the requisite specialist knowledge of their specific departments such as finance, IT, operations, Human Resources (HR), Research and Development (R&D), Training and Development (T&D), and can strategize according to the information and foresight they receive. They can, in turn, coordinate with each other by sharing their strategies and synergizing them so that they are all on the same page with regard to the organization's vision. Ultimately, the CEO will have the final say in aligning all these strategies. They also have broader powers for approving promotions, reassignments, and terminations of other senior leaders within the organization.

The next level in the hierarchy, following the CEOs and the C-Suite officers, are the senior managers, followed by others such as regional managers, site managers, office managers, and departmental managers. Their primary role in the organization is to report directly to the chief executives and aid them in formulating, implementing, and evaluating their strategies. Senior managers have to be in lockstep with the chief executives' strategies as they are the people who will be implementing them on the ground, as well as report back about how effectively or otherwise the strategy is going.

While they do not have as much flexibility to make necessary adjustments in the strategy as the C-suite officers do, senior and department managers have been entrusted to a certain degree to obtain results while staying within the rules and regulations of the organizations and their leaders' vision. Managers have had enough experience under their belts to carry out the leaders' plans, but they also recognize when and where they can question or clarify any agenda as and when needed.

They are also responsible for the maintenance and upkeep of their own individual departments in particular, as well as upgrading technology, recruiting a diverse employee base, soliciting client feedback, focusing on product enhancements and development, contributing and generating new ideas, innovations, and alternatives, setting up departmental objectives, and expanding the organization's operations in line with the chief executives' strategies. Other forms of senior managers and departmental managers include non-commissioned officers, sergeants, and entrepreneurs.

The widest possible tier of leaders is that of the entry-level managers. These include assistant managers, supervisors, team leads, line-leaders, unit leaders, foremen, and the like, and are also the stepping stone for employees with leadership potential to climb up the corporate ladder. The entry or first-level managers are responsible for the day-to-day functioning of an organization. These include, but are not limited to, overseeing operations, directly interacting with employees and team members, ensuring productivity and efficiency, training new employees, preparing reports for senior management, and communicating the directives and strategies as devised by the senior leadership.

For most employees, entry-level managers are the face of the top leadership. Their constant interactions with the employees convey the organization's strategies and goals and build trust and rapport. They take care of any small issues or concerns as long as it is in their power to do so while also consulting with senior managers about concerns over their pay grade. Their knowledge of an organization's day-to-day processes and functions is invaluable, as is their ability to motivate employees and delegate tasks.

Leaders in All but Name

Oftentimes, people associate titles, designations, and ranks with leadership. Naturally, a CEO will come off to any casual observer as a major player, a high-level strategist, and a bold visionary who can spot the potential behind any strategy and put the wheels in motion to carry it out. They are also there to serve as the source of inspiration for their employees and followers with their charisma, vision, decisiveness, and ability to capture everyone's imagination.

By the same token, there are other players who also inspire, motivate, and guide employees to make the vision a reality. The only difference is that they do not obviously appear to be at a level in the hierarchy that automatically says "top leader." These people may not have the title or designation, but they have their own role to play in driving an organization's workforce toward achieving its goals.

These include coaches and mentors who may or may not be a part of the official hierarchy in an organization.

Nevertheless, they serve an important purpose by motivating and guiding employees in a way that top leaders do not do directly. Coaches are responsible for bringing out the best in employees and followers by offering them support, guidance, and motivation. Instead of providing solutions to problems that employees approach them with, like managers and senior managers would, coaches prefer to inspire them to seek out solutions themselves. They possess strong communication and analytical skills that they can use to share feedback with employees and encourage them to see their place in the bigger picture.

On the other hand, mentors share their perspectives and experiences from their time working in a particular organization or industry with other employees — mentees — to inspire them by example. The goal of mentors is to take in employees in whom they see potential leadership material and take them under their wing. By sharing their knowledge, experience, and own career trajectory, as well as counseling them on how to chart out their own professional growth, mentors help employees to see a solid career path that they may not have been able to see before and help them understand what efforts and sacrifices need to be made to achieve that. Positive mentoring helps organizations retain top talent, improve productivity, and carve out a succession plan for elevating new leaders up the hierarchy. Like coaches, mentors should also possess strong communication and analytical skills as well as a great deal of relevant expertise in the industry.

Leaders and organizations can also bring in outside consultants who possess industry-relevant experience and have a proven track record of success. These consultants can be former business owners, leaders, academics, and consultancy groups who advise — or essentially consult with — the senior leadership and management on how to devise corporate strategies and how to make the organization more efficient and productive. Similarly, organizations can also avail the services of corporate planning departments that specialize in devising strategic plans based on the directives of the top leadership.

An often underrated player in the picture is the executive assistant of the CEO. Though the position itself is administrative and not at all high up on the hierarchy, an executive assistant is a direct line to the CEO's office. Anyone who is anyone in an organization who wants to get in touch with the CEO has to go through the executive assistant first and discuss what they will be bringing to the CEO's notice. Executive assistants coordinate activities between the senior leadership and management with the CEO. They are also the CEO's troubleshooters, analysts, and data collectors regarding any particular project, especially the progress of the CEO's vision.

Characteristics of Great Leadership

Leaders have to be decisive first and foremost. They will frequently find themselves in positions where they must always have various solutions to solving a problem. They must then weigh the pros and cons of each solution and the impact it would have on the problem before deciding on which solution is best. They make informed decisions after analyzing all the information they collect while also keeping their emotions in check. This is essential as they may feel a tide of emotions coming in from their followers and employees regarding a particular problem, which is why they need to ensure that they are not caught in the wake. They have to maintain their sense of reason while making critical decisions, as any wrong decision can have detrimental effects on the organization as a whole.

The best place for leaders to start working on how strong their reasoning and decision-making abilities are is to work on their emotional intelligence, focus on personal development, and gain self-awareness. They need to keep their eye on the big picture rather than get caught up in the day-to-day concerns that can distract them.

They should be delegating smaller matters down the chain of command and focusing on achieving the organization's goals through time management, prioritizing the goals as required, and analyzing their strengths, weaknesses, and areas of improvement. Leaders should also recognize that there could be inherent biases that can come between them and reasonable thinking. Therefore, they need to counteract these biases by consulting with their senior leadership and getting feedback regarding any initiatives that may require a different point of view.

Leaders should also remember that, despite their best efforts, there is every chance that things can go wrong. The first thing is to recognize any shortcomings on their part and be ready to accept their mistakes, even if it means doing so in front of their followers. However, they should also bring solutions to any such mistakes so that rather than shattering confidence, leaders are able to retain it. They should also keep their professional and personal lives completely separate so that neither of them interferes with the other. In the case of professional life, any issues taking place at home or in their personal lives can be detrimental to an organization's priorities, particularly in the position a leader is in. But this is where leaders have to show exceptional mental acuity and fortitude to not let any such issues affect their role.

Next, leaders need to set expectations for their followers, not just in terms of their performance but also for their professional development. They encompass the role of managers, trainers, mentors, and coaches all at the same time. They are involved in their employees' development right from the start, i.e., the recruitment stage, looking to build a team from diverse backgrounds and possessing a wide variety of skills and personal qualities. This will allow leaders to instill professional attributes and values in their teams as soon as they start working, as well as develop trust and rapport among each other and set goals and expectations. Offering their teams training and letting them know how far they can make it in the hierarchy is an investment into their future as well as that of the organization.

Leaders also have to act with empathy when it comes to their followers. Rather than come off as authoritative and dictatorial, a leader who exhibits empathy for their followers becomes a tower of strength for the organizations, and they have complete faith in their abilities. They can also rely on leaders to be fair and unbiased when it comes to delegating responsibilities and recognizing their talents, while leaders are going to do the same to build strong and efficient teams.

Clear and comprehensive communication on the leaders' part takes care of a number of things. It conveys the leader's intentions regarding their mission and reinforces the organization's values, not to mention giving and receiving updates regarding the progress of any ongoing goals and projects. Communication is also vital to keep everyone in the loop about any impending problems that leaders foresee. Oftentimes, organizations that do not keep their employees or followers apprised of any problematic situations, such as financial downturns, employee turnover, a decline in output, production, and sales, and so on, create a negative impact in their minds. Employees feel their presence and need in the organization are transactional and are therefore not considered valued.

This breaks down their trust in leaders and, in effect, the organization. This does no favors to the organization as negative word-of-mouth will create a lack of faith in other existing and future employees. Furthermore, if employees do not feel valued and trusted by their leaders, they do not have to stay, nor would they want to give any more effort and creativity to what they would perceive as a lost cause. Therefore, leaders should use positive and proactive communication to develop and maintain trust among the followers in a way that aligns with the organization and shows people that they are trusted, valued, and considered integral parts of the organization.

Keep in mind that communication styles vary depending on the audience. It takes into account the various cultural characteristics of different individuals, departments, personality types, hierarchies, and even strategic business partners. Leaders must consider cross-cultural communication to get their message across effectively while also respecting their audience. They should keep in mind that communication styles over different mediums, such as in-person, over the phone, through electronic media, and so on, require subtlety and nuance, which can be improved over time through empathy and practice. They must also remain enthusiastic, excited, and confident in themselves, which will reflect in their communication. This is important to maintain positivity and optimism among everyone in the organization.

Leaders must show that they are capable of strategic thinking, positive action, and great innovation and must foster these qualities among their followers and employees. In order to do this, leaders must be willing to listen to new ideas with an open mind. They must recognize the growing and constantly evolving business landscape, especially critical aspects such as technological development, changes in laws, rules and regulations, and much more. This way, they can make the necessary changes or adjustments to their strategies appropriately. This is very important to ensure that their strategies remain viable toward realizing the future that they have been focused on.

Leaders must also provide opportunities to their followers and employees to brainstorm new ideas, come up with daring concept designs or prototypes, give input on existing products and services, and allow them to practically test out these ideas in the form of beta or test phases.

Above all else, leaders need to have a sense of responsibility, ethics, and transparency. They must incorporate ethical business practices when dealing with their followers, employees, fellow colleagues, business partners, and the communities most affected by their organization. Leaders must be honest, upright, transparent, and genuine with the people they are dealing with on a consistent basis. They must also take responsibility for their own mistakes instead of assigning blame. However, they must hold people accountable when and where necessary. Rather than covering up their own shortcomings or that of the organization, leaders must be honest with their followers and other members of the hierarchy about what these shortcomings are and how they can best eliminate them.

Leaders Put the Needs of Others Before Their Own

As leaders, selflessness should be a naturally occurring quality. Unlike the military concept where the top leadership or "brass" directs its troops into battle and puts them in a line of fire, leaders in the business world and other fields, such as industry, technology, politics, sports, and so on, prefer to lead from the front in order to inspire their followers and show them that they aren't going to put them in situations that they weren't willing to be put into themselves. When a team is successful, the leader credits the team's efforts; but when a team fails, the leader accepts responsibility for a strategy that fell short of expectations. This way, leaders harbor an atmosphere where their teams feel shielded from any harsh criticism that may come their way in case of any failures.

With this approach, leaders also put the needs of their teams before their own. In today's fast-paced and result-driven business environment, it isn't uncommon for organizations and leaders to push their teams toward achieving goals, often at the expense of their health, mental well-being, and efficiency. This, coupled with the fact that the leader only sees the bottom line rather than inspiring their teams, makes them come across as selfish and inconsiderate.

The best antidote to such an environment is creating an inspiring, motivating, uplifting, and optimistic workplace. This way, leaders show their teams respect, listen to their concerns, offer feedback and constructive criticism, and hold them in high esteem. Nevertheless, leaders must remember to maintain certain boundaries, which means they cannot be outright friends with their team members. Friendly, yes; friends, not necessarily. In order to ensure a successful leader-follower dynamic, it is enough to be inspiring, respectful, and motivating without unnecessarily having to resort to becoming buddies with your followers.

Providing your teams with the necessary tools and resources to do their tasks efficiently and creating a comfortable, non-judgmental, friendly, and appreciative working environment goes a long way to creating a safe workplace where people continue to contribute to the best of their abilities. This environment also provides leaders with the right platform to coach, mentor, and critique their people's performances and remind everyone about the organization's values, traditions, and goals. It will require some correcting on the leaders' part, but the approach has to be constructive rather than punitive. Leaders should be able to differentiate between their people making a mistake simply because they need more help understanding what to do versus people breaking the rules deliberately, and must then act appropriately.

In any case, taking punitive action should only focus on a follower's actions, not the character. No matter how dire the mistake is, no one will appreciate or feel inspired if their character and self are targeted, which can create an environment of hostility for the people. Everyone can see and interpret harsh punitive action as symptomatic of a work culture where the leadership not only doesn't value its people but also aims to devalue them even further. In organizations that do not value diversity and inclusion, top leadership and management have been known to target individuals on racial, gender-based, ethnic, and religious lines whether subtly or overtly. While there are laws in place to protect people from such harassment, these actions are detrimental to people's psychological and emotional well-being, making them fear similar treatment in other work environments.

This is why leaders need to cultivate a safe, protected, and emotionally healthy environment for their people in both a professional and personal capacity. Employees and followers should be able to feel that they can be an active and integral part of the workplace, where their efforts are recognized, and their mistakes are handled in a respectful and corrective manner rather than a punitive one. Furthermore, leaders also need to ensure that their people never feel threatened at a personal level in the organization, especially because of them. They have to be fair, tolerant, and inclusive if they want to foster an environment that welcomes people from all walks of life so that they can add their unique ideas to the mix. People are naturally inclined to perform beyond expectations when they feel that they are in a safe environment free from discrimination and prejudice.

To sum up, leaders are nothing without their people, which is why they must keep a people-centric mindset that puts their needs first. Leaders should definitely focus on their own needs and vision, but it is their people who will help them achieve those goals. By focusing on what will help their people perform at their best and reward their performance appropriately, leaders ensure sustainability and success for the organization as a whole and not just themselves.

CHAPTER

3

AUTHORITY IS NOT THE SAME AS LEADERSHIP

Leadership is the art of getting someone else to do something you want done because he wants to do it. –Dwight D. Eisenhower

A common concept ingrained in nearly everyone from an early age is that leadership is all about being in charge. People follow leaders who have a commanding presence, can lay down the law, and drive them to achieve results. But as we have reviewed in earlier chapters about authoritarian leadership and the 'great man' theory, there is more than one way to inspire confidence and achieve results. Being in charge or having the authority to lead people is just one tool—a major one, but a tool nonetheless.

Though it is not technically leadership, authority has an important function in every aspect of life, from parenting to governing. Everyone has had a leadership moment at some point in life, i.e., any situation where people's attention was squarely on you. It was a moment when your people opened themselves to you, providing them with direction or guidance. So even if you've never spoken publicly, if you spoke with someone and shared a thought, you were leading. The core of leadership is influence and the ability to focus people's attention and efforts to accomplish tasks, which in turn cements a leader's authority.

In this chapter, we will be examining the different types of authority and how authority can be different from leadership while working within the leadership framework.

What Authority Is and Isn't

The word "authority" comes from the Latin *auctor*, meaning "master, author, and leader" (WordSense, n.d.). As the name suggests, authority is either a given or a stated responsibility a person has over other people, resources, or procedures. In a corporate or professional environment, authority represents power, respect, responsibility, and accountability. Though it may be a core ingredient in leadership, authority instills a different idea in followers where they believe that they are duty-bound to be of service and loyal to authority figures. This can be witnessed in the most basic examples of authority, such as parents over children, coaches over players, teachers over students, priests over disciples, etc.

For instance, both parents hold their authority over a child once the child is born. The mother is responsible for the child's health, nourishment, and well-being, while the father is usually responsible for the child's welfare, education, expenses, and so on, though these roles are interchangeable to a certain degree. But while parents carry out their responsibilities for the child's welfare, it does not make all their decisions unquestionable, particularly if they do not consider the child's best interests, such as letting them pursue skills and talents that they are good at.

While authority can instill a sense of loyalty and responsibility among the followers, it is not enough without the other core ingredients of successful leadership, such as inspiration, motivation, empathy, and communication. Following the lifting of COVID-19 restrictions, the phenomena of the "Great Resignation" and "quiet quitting" have shown that employees are no longer interested or committed to working for an organization or leadership that does not value or appreciate their hard work and loyalty. The most obvious indicators of job dissatisfaction that are at the core of these phenomena are taxing working conditions, unreasonable demands for flexibility, unfair salaries or remuneration, and an obvious lack of motivation from leadership and management. If anything, the overwhelming opinion is that employees can no longer tolerate working for an organization or leadership that does not give them the space to grow or feel happy and motivated to give their all.

This reveals an alarming trait among the leaders of today: They are relying more and more on authority to ensure that their people are working hard, but they are not leading them to realize their full potential. It makes the work employees are doing feel redundant, repetitive, and mechanical as if they were cogs in a machine that resets every day. Moreover, most employees assume that anyone in a position of authority knows what they are doing and that they are looking out for the organization's best interests. However, if someone is only using their authority to simply get work done rather than motivate or inspire the workforce, the employees and followers won't know if it is the right thing to do or not.

While the essence of quiet quitting stems from a challenge of what traditional corporate America deems necessary for success, such as requiring working in an office and attending meetings, the formal and professional title and reasoning are "working to rule." This signifies that workers are only willing to perform tasks and responsibilities specifically outlined and required by management within the prescribed working hours they are legally and contractually hired for.

On the other hand, leaders do not hesitate to remind their people of how important they are and how much their efforts contribute to the organization's overall success, which benefits them in the long run. This is how genuine leaders look out for the organization's best interests which are directly tied to the welfare and happiness of its employees.

Though leaders at the top of the hierarchy understand how their people must be treated in order to have them perform at their best, managers who directly supervise the people are more interested in the day-to-day running of the organization. Due to this, managers can inadvertently create a toxic working culture that leads to low employee retention and high training costs. Therefore, leaders have to remind the direct line managers responsible for employee welfare to act beyond their given authority. They can do so by using their own authority to empower the direct line managers down the hierarchy to exercise and espouse the same leadership qualities that they do. This way, managers will be able to use their authority effectively by assigning tasks, directing resources, and making decisions while at the same time reminding their people of how their hard work, dedication, and loyalty are being appreciated and even rewarded.

Types of Authority

According to an essay titled *The Three Types of Legitimate Rule*, German sociologist Max Weber laid out the concept of authority in three different segments, which would then classify a leader's particular style of authority (Weber & Whimster, 2009). The first is traditional authority, which is based on the various social customs and traditions of different societies. Most developed societies have, at one point or another, had a Monarchy as a traditional authority system which is still enforced today. In traditional authority, followers obey without question and accept the authority figure as infallible. Traditional authority relies on the follower's deference, respect, and total submission . There have been rare cases when traditional authority figures have been challenged, such as the Russian Revolution against the Romanov Empire. In Weber's own words, traditional authority is the "authority of the eternal yesterday," which imposes inequalities over the followers so that the authority figures remain in power forever.

The second type of authority is rational or legal authority. Rational authority emphasizes a natural legitimacy and succession model, such as military hierarchies, democratic elections, and corporate organization lines. In rational authority, an individual or group has been legally selected to be ruling authority figures, changing in order of succession or through a vote. Each authority figure moves up a hierarchy based on their experience, skills, and expertise and receives additional powers along the way. Once one authority figure leaves, they no longer have the same authority, and it is passed on to the next person in line through "rationally created rules" as Weber pointed out.

Rational authority is a direct opponent to traditional authority. One of the key differences between the two is that a follower can challenge a person in a rational authority structure. This is particularly true in situations where followers offer constructive criticism of any decision that they feel may not be in line with the organization's best interests. In such a scenario, rational authority figures may either accept the criticism or debate it with their point of view as well as any specific knowledge that they have.

As per Max Weber (2009), the third and final type of authority is charismatic authority. Unlike traditional and rational authority, in which followers have no choice but to defer to the authority figures, they do so in charismatic authority because they want to; and they want to because they believe in the leader. Leaders with charismatic authority inspire their followers with their confidence, charm, energy, charisma, and magnetism while buckling against tradition, convention, and rules.

Major world leaders have used their magnetic personalities and charismatic authority to capture the imagination of their followers to create lasting effects, both positive and negative. While Martin Luther King, Jr., Winston Churchill, Nelson Mandela, John F. Kennedy, and Mahatma Gandhi have ushered in waves of social change and upheaval, dictators such as Adolf Hitler, Benito Mussolini, Idi Amin, and the like have also created models of repressive and totalitarian states which had been welcomed only due to their charisma and magnetism. The 21st century has also seen similar waves of upheaval by leaders such as Barack Obama and Donald Trump, both of whom rallied support with their charismatic authority.

In the business world, many pioneers have also used charismatic authority to instill loyalty, dedication, and enthusiasm over the years. A lot of modern-day technology giants, such as Bill Gates, Steve Jobs, Elon Musk, Jeff Bezos, Mark Zuckerberg, Richard Branson, and the like, are also great examples of positive charismatic authority. At the same time, there are also examples of negative charismatic authority, such as Elizabeth Holmes and Martin Shkreli, who also captured the imagination of their followers, but ultimately used their personalities to become famous for all the wrong reasons.

Charismatic authority has proven to be more than enough for leaders to captivate their followers and the world at large, which often puts the need for ability, experience, and knowledge on the back burner. But as Weber puts it, there will come a time when the latter qualities will be required, which is when leaders will have to show their followers that they are up to the task. But if a leader with charismatic authority cannot justify their position to their followers, they will lean on traditional and rational authority structures to retain control. Ironically, it is these two authority types that charismatic authority is supposed to be bucking against, as it suggests that the traditional and rational authority structures restrict out-of-the-box thinking and innovation.

In another instance, controversial American social psychologist Stanley Milgram observed in his obedience experiments (Milgram, 2010) that the concept of authority compelled people to follow anyone who wielded it, even to unconscionable lengths. These experiments were influenced by the horrors of the Holocaust, where the dogma of "simply following orders" was seen as a recurring theme in the command and control structure of the Nazi regime. Milgram was particularly taken by the trial of Adolf Eichmann, the man responsible for every aspect of the organization of the Holocaust, including the deportation, transportation, dehumanization, and mass extermination of the Jewish population of German-occupied Europe in the early 20th century. While the Nazi elite prioritized the "Final Solution" in Nazi terminology, Eichmann laid the groundwork for making it a reality. This showed just how fanatically followers can be devoted to an idea once it is laid down by the authority figures as a matter of immense importance.

Based on these experiments, Milgram observed that there were eight different types of authority among people in power. The first is founder authority which, as the name suggests, belongs to the person who has founded a group, company, organization, movement, etc. They are highly invested and involved in the activities, direction, progress, and outcomes of the group. They also have relevant experience in managing large groups of people and assigning them specific responsibilities. Therefore, their authority encompasses every level of the group or organization's hierarchy, including the senior leadership.

The next type is ownership authority. Again, this is found in people who are owners of a business or organization, particularly small and medium businesses and manufacturers. Because of their controlling interest, business owners have the exclusive right to make decisions for the organization, both internally and externally. This exclusive decision-making power affects everyone in the group directly as they may not have any platform to vote against any decisions that could be risky or lead to undesirable consequences. People with ownership authority must be decisive, possess strong business acumen, and be receptive to feedback from their people. This will not guarantee that they will take this feedback into consideration, which means that they will direct the organization's priorities how they see fit. Ownership authority can exist in businesses as small as mom-and-pop stores, sole proprietor businesses such as event managers, logistics providers, small-scale industrial manufacturers, franchise owners, and as high up as owners of major sports teams.

Not unlike ownership authority, relational authority also entails that a leader's actions may affect the entire group. The only difference is that the member does not have to be the owner. The member could be in any of the leadership levels in the hierarchy, but their decisions can directly impact the group's efforts, essentially derailing them if their actions do not pan out. Instances of relational authority can be observed among sports teams where if one person does not perform as expected or meets their goals, the whole team suffers. An infamous example of this is when NBA legend Scottie Pippen refused to play the last 1.8 seconds of the third game in the playoffs between the Chicago Bulls and the New York Knicks in 1994.

Though the game ended in a victory for the Bulls, Pippen's decision caused a scene where the team felt demoralized. His standing in the team as the most respectable player and best performer of that season following the retirement of Michael Jordan meant that everyone on the team looked up to him to lead. By Pippen's own admission in the latest years, his actions were fueled by the decision of the Bulls' coach, Phil Jackson, who decided to let fellow Bulls teammate Tony Kukoč take the match-winning shot. Both these decisions show how relational authority can affect a group's trajectory as well as its morale.

This event highlights how any person in a group, no matter the hierarchy, be it peers, supervisors, leaders, coaches, and so on, is connected to each other and has relational authority over one another.

Reward authority and punitive authority are two contrasting types, with their ideas on opposite ends of the spectrum. That doesn't mean that the two ideas aren't used interchangeably when needed. In reward authority, leaders prefer rewarding positive behavior and actions of the group. These rewards could be material rewards such as pay bonuses, awards, titles, sterling performance reviews that go in the file, prizes such as a weekend getaway or a free dinner at an upscale restaurant, and salary increments. They could also be verbal, such as praise and recognition, or even non-verbal expressions, such as a pat on the back. Examples of reward authority include roles such as teachers, educators, HR professionals, coaches, and parents.

Alternatively, leaders may also rely on punitive authority, where they could withhold the rewards in the case of negative behavior or actions, or they could punish people for the same reason. These negative actions could be making small errors, not following the rules, or even having conflicting opinions with the authority figure. While the above examples of roles also hold true for punitive authority, more substantial roles include people in positions of legal importance, such as judges, magistrates, and law enforcement officials.

Both reward and punitive authority lead to results where people who work hard and achieve their targets are rewarded with positions of power. Most entry-level managers have benefited directly from their performance as a non-manager by being promoted for their hard work, successes, and unique skills. Similarly, existing managers who have shown great results are trusted to deliver on a wide variety of projects. This means that they can be given projects with a greater scope that are of higher significance to the organization's vision with the expectation that they will repeat the same formula for success. Such authority requires strategic planning, coordinating organizational efforts, and timely execution.

Building up experience and insights in a particular field creates expert authority. These people specialize in a certain area, perhaps a couple more, such as psychology, economics, ethics, law, medicine, politics, and so on. People with expert power tend to be called upon as corporate consultants, political analysts, and expert witnesses in trials. Their expert knowledge in the area makes them ideal for providing invaluable insights and also offering course corrections in case an organization is not heading in the right direction.

The last of Milgram's types of authority is reverent authority. This type of authority is usually channeled through personal qualities such as kindness, compassion, respect, and empathy rather than any professional skills or talents, though those are also part of the package. While people with reverent authority don't have to be experts, they do have to be good at caring for other people and their needs. Examples of reverent authority figures include counselors, psychiatrists, and priests or clerics.

The above types show leaders what authority traits they themselves embody and what the outcomes of their actions and decisions might be if they abide by these traits. Nevertheless, if the actions lead to an outcome that puts the rest of the group or an organization at risk, such as in ownership, punitive, and relational authorities, then it will not create a sense of devotion among the group to the leader and instead can create an atmosphere of distrust, demotivation, and despair. At the same time, if the leader's actions and decisions lead to positive outcomes as well as praise, recognition, care, empathy, and rewards, such as in reward and reverent authorities, the dynamic between leaders and followers grows stronger and more trusting.

Also, the hallmark of great leadership is knowing to delegate authority as and when needed. This shows people that they can be trusted and empowered to work on tasks based on their judgment and temperament as long as it is achieving the desired results. Not only does delegation relieve some of the pressures of responsibility from the leader's shoulders, but it also shows which of the group has the right set of skills, qualities, and decisiveness to take action, thus putting them on the leader's watchlist for people who have great leadership potential ahead. Furthermore, the fact that leaders are able to trust others with responsibilities and delegate makes people feel that they can voice their ideas and concerns when called for. This is important as it creates a conducive and cooperative working environment where a variety of opinions are welcomed.

It is also important because if authority is only exercised by leaders, then the people within the groups miss out on opportunities to develop problem-solving skills themselves. In such cases, leaders should always encourage their people to not just come to them with problems but also with the solutions to those problems, i.e., how they would solve them if they could. The beauty of this approach is that leaders can encourage their followers to think for themselves and present their own ideas on how they would approach a problem. Leaders can then either agree with their ideas or offer them constructive feedback on how the idea can be refined based on the wider strategies and vision of the organization. Either way, leaders will be able to empower and embolden their people to become more creative and proactive.

With the right kind of authority that fosters collaboration, leaders can create a working environment that emphasizes teamwork, inclusion, building rapport, and a sense of belonging. While they can use their authority to keep things in order and to establish a chain of command, real leadership is appreciated when followers can trust and respect the people above them based on their integrity, decisiveness, and knowledge.

This is why great leaders need to use different kinds of authority instead of sticking to one type. Using varying kinds of authority as the situation demands it, such as using reward authority in one instance and punitive in the other, leaders cultivate ideal working conditions that are both fair and firm. People can then see that their leaders are going to act according to positive and negative situations with varying kinds of authority as well as effective management techniques.

Authority vs. Leadership

Knowing the difference between authority and leadership is not easy. In fact, the line between the two is pretty much drawn in the sand since both concepts depend on each other to push the wheels forward. Leaders should be able to differentiate between the two, especially if they plan on taking a more active role in the workplace. The most important distinction to make is that authority can be earned or legitimized as per the rules and laws of the environment. Once it is, the authority figures can exercise it over their followers by giving instructions or orders, using their power to get their way, and quash any opposition or questions.

The Trump presidency and the fallout of the 2020 U.S. presidential election is a major example of how an authority figure has exercised tremendous power not just over the state institutions and members of their own political parties, but among the hearts and minds of a major segment of American society in a way like never before. A businessman and celebrity with no prior government or military experience took the highest office in the country on a wave of overwhelming support by a far-right majority. His vicious tirades in public appearances, where he put forward his polarizing and conservative viewpoints over key issues such as race, gender, abortion, immigration, and much more, as well as similar thoughts through his now banned Twitter account, created a hostile and shocking environment that saw unprecedented hatred for all things the US had achieved in its history.

This all came to a head when Trump tweeted about how the 2020 election had been "stolen" by Democrats and candidate Joe Biden, which led to Trump lighting the fire under a highly charged rally outside the White House on January 6, 2021, the day Congress met to certify the results of the 2020 elections and Biden's victory. But the rally turned violent as Trump supporters stormed the Capitol, resulting in five deaths and the evacuation of lawmakers from the building. Though Trump was impeached on charges of insurrection, the January 6 attack on the Capitol summarizes how authority can be abused and create disastrous circumstances.

Keep in mind that as this authority is earned or legitimized, the people in charge have the right to use it as they see fit, with the expectation that they will have the necessary foresight to do what is best in a given situation. This is referred to as the positional attribute, i.e., utilizing authority as it comes with the role of a leader.

But does this mean that the actions and decisions taken by leaders inspire loyalty among their followers? Have leaders been able to cultivate a positive working environment by relying solely on punitive authority? Do followers feel that their contributions make any difference in the presence of the founder or ownership authorities?

Authority, much like anything else in leadership, is a tool. What makes authority such a versatile tool is not just how leaders choose to use it but also how they can empower their followers with it. Instead of being all about ordering and micromanaging, great leaders should use authority to involve, inspire, and encourage their people to live up to their full potential in the guise of managing them. This is known as the personal attribute, which, unlike the positional attribute, puts the spotlight on the personality traits that leaders have and use. Whereas people in a group would simply respect the authority as it comes with the leader's position, the personal attribute ensures that people respect their character instead. Leaders should also be approachable whenever their people have any issues that need to be communicated.

One of the characteristics of the positional attribute is ordering people to complete tasks. This is part and parcel of what a leader is supposed to do, but that isn't the only approach they can take. Giving orders may have its merits whenever required; however, it only shows followers that leaders only care about the bottom line. But leaders participating shoulder to shoulder with their followers, on the other hand, creates a positive impression in the group. It becomes obvious to them that their leaders are ready and willing to take on the challenge themselves and lead them by example instead of giving commands. Rubbing shoulders with their group also gives leaders a first-hand situation report about the group's progress, strengths and weaknesses, and areas of improvement.

Aside from leading by example, participation also shows that leaders exhibit humility rather than pride. Most leaders are expected by their followers to be high-and-mighty and not bothered with matters down on terra firma, especially those with founder, ownership, or punitive authority. The feeling is similar among leaders who prefer managing rather than leading. In their minds, they are the person with the solutions and do not need to listen to their groups and their opinions. Such leaders cannot help but rely completely on using authority as their default setting because they do not want their authority and role to be undermined if their groups start having opinions of their own, especially those that stand in direct contradiction to the leader.

To make matters worse, such leaders rarely acknowledge any of their team's hard work and successes and instead portray any successes as their own. This is the kind of arrogance that creates bitterness and passive-aggressive behavior among the team. They feel that if their hard work and creativity have no value, then they may as well not bother working at all, resulting in procrastination, inefficiency, and contributing to a negative working environment. This is why leaders have to be humble — so that they do not feel like enemies to their groups. However, they should also remember to be assertive rather than arrogant whenever they feel they need to remind everyone about their authority.

In conclusion, leaders can create a positive, open, and collaborative work environment by using their authority to inspire and build trust. Both leadership skills and authority have to work in sync so that the organization can have clear communication, opportunities to contribute new ideas, and can also work together towards achieving the organization's goals.

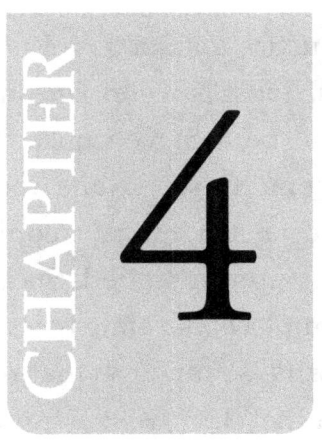

4

TRUST—THE KEY TO INFLUENCE

The trust of the people in the leaders reflects the confidence of the leaders in the people. –Paulo Freire

A sk yourself this: Who do you trust? Do you trust your spouse, your children, your doctor, your priest? Do you trust your therapist to keep your secrets no matter what? Do you trust your mechanic not to fleece you with shoddy work? Do you trust your accountant to have all your books in order? If yes, then why? What is it that they do that makes you want to trust their judgment, words, and actions completely? Is it because of their abilities and talents? Is it because they are highly skilled and capable at their job? Or is it something more?

Trust is an essential component in every single living creature. Children and offspring trust their parents to look out for them, animals trust their instincts for survival, and people trust the laws and justice to take its course to safeguard their rights and interests. Trust is a simple contract that implies a certain outcome will be achieved once the required efforts are made. People come to work, and they get paid. People work hard, and they get bonuses. People make a mistake, and they expect to be reprimanded. Such trust mechanisms should already be in place, but time has shown that trust can be broken rather easily, so much so that the one thing people now trust is the fact that their trust is fragile.

In such an environment, it is crucial for leaders to show that they can be trusted to look out for the best interests of their people. But it isn't an easy proposition when there is an established history of exploitation, dominance, and control exercised by leaders for their own benefit. This chapter aims to establish the importance of building trust so that leaders can generate a sense of loyalty and dedication among their teams, not out of obligation but out of mutual respect and admiration.

Developing Trust In Leadership

There is more to influencing people than simply being authoritative and charismatic. Leaders also need to get people to believe in their abilities to lead. They need people to see who their leaders are, what kind of leadership style they fancy, what values and priorities are important to them, what their expectations are, and how far they are willing to go for their people. They also want to know more about how their leaders will treat them when things go right or if they go wrong. Will their leaders be punitive? Will they help them understand their mistakes and counsel them on what corrective course they need to take? Or will they even take on a vindictive position?

Trust isn't just something that people need to have in their leaders. It is a fundamental human requirement that everyone wants to fulfill. This is especially true for leaders and their followers, regardless of which of them you are. You want to do your best to make sure that your purpose, and that of your team, leaders, and organization, is aligned towards mutually agreed goals. In order to accomplish this, you need to be able to collaborate with each other so that you can deliver your best performance. But collaboration can only take place when trust between both parties is present. Conversely, it is nearly impossible for people to see eye to eye with the organization and its leadership when there is no trust present. This leaves organizations in an unpredictable and vulnerable position.

In modern leadership, it isn't just enough for leaders to achieve goals and tasks. Leaders are no longer only defined by the strides that they make. They are also recognized for the way they lead their people. Leaders can deliver incredible innovation and value for their shareholders all they want; however, it won't mean much when they are not respected or seem to have no integrity from the viewpoint of their followers. Leaders need to have integrity and appear to be genuine to their followers so that they can inspire and influence them. This is why leaders must focus on building better trust between themselves and their followers. This is an essential requirement for them to develop their businesses and organizations. Leaders cannot achieve great strides by themselves. They need to have the confidence and loyalty of a team of dedicated professionals. However, even the most dedicated professionals can only go so far to help leaders achieve their vision. This is where trust plays a very important role.

Leaders can begin developing trust by possessing unimpeachable integrity. For this, leaders must come up with realistic goals and expectations that they then lay out for their followers in an environment of mutual collaboration, fairness, and respect. Leaders must be honest with what they expect from their people and the challenges that lie in front of them. If leaders are straightforward and sincere about what their people can expect in various projects and initiatives and how they will be tested, they can then earn the loyalty of their people, who will be more than committed to going the extra mile to achieve those goals and expectations.

This, in turn, highlights another major quality that leaders need to develop trust, and that is the strength of their character. Leaders must say what they mean and mean what they say when it comes to taking their team members into confidence. If they say that they are committed to making this a collaborative relationship, then they need to be there alongside their people, offering them guidance, insights, resources, and motivation so that the people are ready and willing to do what is necessary to achieve the goals. At the same time, leaders must also be present and take responsibility when things go wrong. Even though it is the people who are responsible for executing strategies, it is the leaders who have developed and convinced their people of said strategies and must accept their part if and when any of these strategies go sour.

A great example of this is an event that took place in 1979 when the Indian Space Research Organization's (ISRO) first efforts to launch a Satellite Launch Vehicle (SLV-III) were met with failure. The project was headed by Dr. APJ Abdul Kalam, who spoke at length in 2013 about the project's failure. The countdown was put on automatic hold by the computer with only 40 seconds to spare, but Kalam's team recommended that they proceed with the launch. Kalam agreed and went ahead with the launch, which failed in the second stage of liftoff. Nevertheless, it was the ISRO's then-chief, Satish Dhawan, who accepted complete responsibility for the incident in a press conference. According to Kalam (Express Web Desk, 2019), Dhawan stated, "Dear friends, we have failed today. I want to support my technologists, my scientists, my staff, so that next year they succeed."

Dhawan's words and actions proved to be exactly what the team needed to build complete trust between them and the chief. The following year, Kalam's team successfully launched the next Satellite Launch Vehicle, Rohini-RS1, into orbit. Only this time, Dhawan put Kalam forward to speak to the press regarding the project's success. In 2013, Kalam recounted how "when failure occurred, the leader of the organization (Dhawan) owned that failure. When success came, he gave it to his team." Kalam's career flourished afterward as he became known as the "Missile Man of India" for his involvement in aerospace as well as missile development. However, one can only speculate what career path he would have taken if

Dhawan had not given that press conference. Kalam became India's 11th President from 2001 to 2007 and passed away in 2015 at the age of 83.

The lesson learned from Dhawan's press conference is that leaders must be ready to accept harsh criticism from different quarters, such as clients, investors, and other stakeholders. But when leaders are ready to take on this criticism and accept it, it will show their people that their trust in their leaders has not gone unrewarded. Such actions by leaders will inspire their people to go back to the drawing board and work even harder so that there is no chance of failure.

While integrity and strength of character are both admirable qualities, leaders must also utilize the talents that they are good at to the best of their ability. Naturally, no team member will follow a leader who is incapable of doing the job that they have asked their followers to do. People need to learn by example, and leaders must set that example from the get-go by showing them how things are done and providing them with necessary feedback and constructive criticism on how to get things done the right way. At the same time, leaders are also responsible for evaluating the progress of their people so that they can determine whether things are going according to plan or if there needs to be some kind of calibration.

The more leaders are present and accessible to their people, the greater the trust they can build. People need to see their leaders up front and in action in order to understand that they are as fully invested in the project as they expect their team to be. This is the preferred method rather than watching their leaders sit behind a desk in offices, watching the world from a fishbowl. Leaders cannot risk being disconnected from the hub of all activity which is why their presence among their team inspires confidence and shows credibility. It also reassures people that they have leaders who are supportive and dependable so that they can approach them whenever something goes wrong or whenever they need guidance. Through this process of building trust, leaders can also develop their sense of empathy and connect with their people at a more human level. This will help them become more appreciative of their people's work and recognize their talent.

Building Influence Through Trust

The distinction between trust and influence isn't a great one. In fact, one can say that trust is a central component of developing influence among people. When leaders are able to develop a great deal of trust among their followers, they can then use their abilities to influence and change their team's behavior so that they follow them toward a certain goal or outcome. This influence can be built by appealing to their people's values, behaviors, attitudes, and priorities.

One very important thing to remember about influence is that it is not the same as power or control. Leaders who influence their people do so in an environment of mutual trust, respect, and empathy. They have achieved this level of influence by getting to know their people and their strengths, weaknesses, aspirations, and priorities. This is a completely different approach from exercising power to manipulate their people toward achieving certain goals. Power is not the best quality to get things done, especially when leaders are looking to build lasting relationships with their teams. Anyone can be coerced or dictated into performing certain tasks, prioritizing certain goals, and achieving certain targets. However, doing so with an absence of trust, respect, and empathy not only leads to half-hearted efforts on the part of followers but can also create an environment where people do not see themselves as valued and trusted enough to remain working for such an organization for long.

In order for leaders to leverage the trust they have built into successfully influencing their people, they must have the right attitude and outlook that is brimming with positivity and optimism. Leaders must be able to show their followers that they have an incredibly positive outlook not just toward their organization but also toward life in general. This will help followers see how motivated leaders are about themselves so that they can incorporate the same attitude among themselves. Once leaders have the right kind of attitude, they will then be able to see not just how they can benefit themselves but also how they can benefit their followers, especially their professional lives and careers.

Leaders can develop a great deal of influence once they let their followers know what they can do to make their lives better. This isn't just related to monetary compensation or career growth opportunities. It is also about professional development, skill enhancement and nurturing, and creating a more fulfilling work role for their people. Leaders who emphasize the need to do what is best for their people directly create an attitude among their followers that will want them to reciprocate towards the positive development of the organization and for the achievement of the leader's vision. This way, leaders can also build positive connections between themselves and their people, which can then be used to get them involved in future projects with the same enthusiasm and zeal, as well as ignite their passion in the same way as that of the leaders.

Furthermore, influence shouldn't just be limited to leaders to their followers. It should also be the other way around. This can be achieved through openness between leaders and followers that is built during the trust development phase. Leaders should encourage a culture of welcoming feedback and observations of their ideas and vision so that they can synchronize it with how their followers can best execute them while keeping the core outcome of their vision intact.

In January 2021, mutual influence building took on a completely new face in the event known as the January 2021 Short Squeeze of Gamestock. The floundering video game retailer had been all but bankrupt in the vein of Blockbuster and Toys R Us when a major action by a group of retail, or individual, investors came together on a social media platform to drive the stock price of Gamestock "to the moon." Fundamentally, such a thing should not even happen as Gamestock's value was floundering in the double digits. But all it took was the efforts of a Reddit group called "WallStreetBets" to shoot the price up so much that it shined a beacon to major investors and financial moguls.

The highlight of this mass action was a one-word tweet that said "Gamestonk!!" in affirmation of the battle cry sounded by WallStreetBets as well as other social media influencers across Twitter, TikTok, Reddit, YouTube, and what-have-you. As a result, Gamestock's price shot up by 1,500% in just two weeks, completely flying in the face of logic, common sense, and traditionally held market dynamics. It became the highest-valued company, albeit temporarily, on the Russell 2000 index on January 28, 2021 (Lipschultz, 2021).

This event signifies how a grassroots level of counter-culture influencers and experts were able to influence a significant number of people to band together to create a landmark event where existing business dynamics and traditions were challenged. It defied the predictions of experts and dramatically impacted the way investors began viewing the market, so much so that major business leaders such as Elon Musk joined the fray in order to multiply its effects.

It goes without saying that a central requirement of influence is building trust. And by trust, we mean genuine trust. A great place to start building trust is within themselves, i.e., the leaders. Oftentimes, leaders have led themselves toward failure due to a lack of confidence in their own leadership skills and abilities. Due to this, such leaders resort to control, power, and intimidation tactics to get their followers to do what they want. This is where leaders need to remind themselves of why they became leaders in the first place and trust their own abilities. At the same time, they should welcome input from their followers and fellow leaders to refine their goals and vision.

Another requirement for influence is for leaders to be transparent about their expectations. This means that leaders need to be clear about their expectations, deadlines, deliverables, progress checkpoints, performance metrics, and more. If leaders leave any kind of ambiguity in their expectations, they risk their followers misinterpreting—and ultimately failing at—their expectations.

Leaders should also carefully evaluate which of their people are high and low performers. But instead of focusing their energy, time, and efforts on the high performers, as certain leaders are going to do, great leaders must provide equal focus towards their high and low performers. This ensures that everyone is performing up to the mark and that the low performers are getting the necessary attention and help they need to excel at their careers. This will show that leaders are not just in it to back the winning horse but would rather have a great team of high-performing individuals all the way, emphasizing how inclusive, patient, and understanding they are. Leaders should also be ready to empower people who they believe can be trusted to wield such authority.

Influence and Social Media

In the last decade or so, social media has proven to be a valuable tool for creating influencers in the literal sense. Social media influencers have become modern-day celebrities in all walks of life, from lifestyle, fashion, technology, religion, and even business. Influencers with large-scale audiences or followers establish new trends and make or break brands, companies, products, and services. One simple post on Instagram can generate a wave of interest in any particular product or service across the globe, thanks to the influencer's endorsement.

This environment is ideal for leaders as they seek to establish their presence and reputation in a larger, more expansive, and dynamic market that is growing increasingly conscious about their right to choose. However, this is also fueled by their desire to be "trending" or to avoid the "Fear Of Missing Out" (FOMO). Most influencers could have tens of thousands of followers that keep increasing; however, their messages are mostly superficial and do not contribute towards a great change, such as helping society, saving the environment, fighting for a cause, and so on.

Leaders are different, though. Their purpose is to inspire change and motivate people to act positively and productively.

Their experience in building success in their organizations by building trust among their people proves that, within their ecosystems, leaders can push people to deliver results and bring about lasting changes. This is why social media can be a valuable tool for leaders to garner widespread support from people around the world toward their cause and vision. In a similar logistical vein to how former US President Donald Trump captured the imagination of the American people by using a wider social media profile as well as a focused social media strategy, leaders can develop, increase, and use their social media presence to appeal to like-minded people towards positive growth and change, unlike Trump's message.

Moreover, with the dynamics of advertising and marketing now heavily relying on social media influencers to offer ringing endorsements for their products, leaders must also look to use this tool for the growth of their business, which is ultimately their larger mission. Through social media, leaders have their finger on the pulse of the people as they take in valuable feedback from clients. This helps companies and brands improve their products, services, and marketing strategies in almost real-time, as well as address the issues highlighted by their customer base.

Even so, leaders remain apprehensive about building their social media presence. Statistics suggest that around 70% of CEOs do not have any kind of personal social media presence on any major platform (Cohen, 2012). Most CEOs cite that social media is distracting, requires greater attention, and also opens them to the potential risk of being openly criticized in an external ecosystem. This applies to both old and young

CEOs. Nevertheless, the hallmark of a great leader is to take any kind of criticism in their stride, especially if it can help them look inward and devise better methods and processes.

With an active social media presence, leaders can leverage their professional credentials to build trust among outside parties, including existing and potential clients, and their detractors. It puts leaders front and center in case there is a wave of negative publicity and opinion about a brand or organization. As responsible leaders, they can use social media to put forward their positions with a carefully considered and perceptive approach. This will help them influence both their supporters and detractors to varying extents and also make them more accessible.

At the heart of a leader's social media presence is the need to be the face of their organization. This means being the biggest advocates and endorsers of their products, services, goals, and vision to get a buy-in from a wide variety of people, who then turn into followers and loyalists. Ultimately, leaders have to consider the growth of the business first, and any method or platform that allows them to generate mass interest in their brand has to be explored. Furthermore, leaders can use social media to enrich the lives of people who aren't their employees. This can be accomplished through motivational messages, personal anecdotes, stories of success and failure, and the various challenges they have been through in their lives. This shows that leaders are not figures to be revered but are, in fact, more human than they had ever been perceived to be.

Additionally, social media can also help leaders understand more about their own employees. Once they open the floodgates to allow communication from all quarters, leaders can get first-hand insights into how their people feel about working for them. Though most employees will be wary of what they say to their leaders on social media, leaders can still find out indirectly from third parties about the working condition of their employees as well as their level of motivation. This can help leaders get in touch with the demands of their people and address these concerns in an open environment to show that they wish to create a positive, encouraging, and welcoming work environment.

This will help leaders to create a positive image of themselves and their organization where people are assured that their hard work, creativity, and dedication are paying off. Through social media, leaders can highlight how amazing it is to work with them, emphasizing on "with" and not "for" as they seek to build lasting trust among their people. They highlight the fact that their employees are a valued part of the organization and that their success is the organization's success.

Your Feedback Counts

Please, leave a REVIEW wherever you made your purchase.

Share your experience with
others help us grow our audience.

 Booksprout

For the opportunity to read advanced copies of our
books, join our review team on BookSprout:

https://booksprout.co/reviewer/team/
31264/panterax-book-review-team

SELF-DISCIPLINE—THE KEY TO BEING A GOOD LEADER

Knowing others is intelligence, knowing yourself is true wisdom. Mastering others is strength, mastering yourself is true power. –Lao Tzu

People in leadership positions at any level of the hierarchy want their teams to perform and grow to the best of their abilities. To ensure this, leaders take the time to understand what makes each of their people tick, including their motivation, history, strengths and weaknesses, and personality traits, in the hopes of matching the right people for the right jobs. It gives them an edge when assigning tasks to people based on their temperament, abilities, and past experience in delivering results.

But how often do leaders look inward? Do they question their motivation, their drive, and their personality traits? Do they wonder why they possess a certain leadership or authority type? And how can they continue to strengthen their leadership style?

This chapter will help you understand how self-discipline is an essential, though generally intimidating, ingredient towards successful leadership. It is a set of principles that are worked upon over time to create productive and lasting habits within leaders. These are ultimately reflected in their leadership styles and abilities. This chapter will also help you look inwards and find out what your true self is like so that you can better connect with the people who follow you.

Know Yourself Before Knowing Others

Leaders often identify themselves as the sum of their roles in the organization or the branding of the organization itself. People who work their way up the corporate ladder could be said to embody the organization's values to a T. But while a person may be able to influence their groups whenever they become managers, supervisors, and so on, it requires a lot more to motivate and inspire them by connecting with their beliefs, values, and desires. In order to achieve this, leaders must first get to know themselves and their own desires, beliefs, and values, as well as their own strengths, weaknesses, and motivations.

Knowing yourself before you know your people and other partners is important as you get a better understanding of your vision and goals. Only then will you be able to sell them on the same goals that you want to achieve, not to mention the same values that you want them to adapt to. But it isn't that simple. It requires time to reflect on who you are, what you have gone through, why you've made the choices you did, where you have sought out opportunities, what makes you happy or sad, and what you hope to achieve. By taking stock of the life you have led, you can analyze what went well, what could have been done better, and what can be changed. This is a continuous process as your professional and personal life progresses into different territory with each passing day. This means that it will require constant reevaluation on your part to gain a better sense of self-awareness, develop better discipline, and refine your character traits.

This process is an investment that leaders make in themselves, which in turn becomes an investment for their people. Once leaders know who they are well enough, they will be able to become more approachable, more trustworthy, and more compassionate to their groups than they had been before. Of course, there is every chance that taking on this journey can reveal things about yourself that you will not like. Quiet introspection is known to be unpredictable and full of surprises, particularly when you come across thoughts you had never imagined you were capable of, both good and bad. Leaders prefer to be involved in the action and the thick of things, but when the time comes to do some quiet reflection, they feel out of their depth, even if it is their own mind that they are taking a swim in. They would rather take challenges head-on and push themselves to achieve their objectives than recognize their own problems, faults, doubts, or vulnerabilities. Instead, they would simply bury it and continue along as if nothing is wrong, when in fact, those very things impact their mentality and decision-making process a lot more than they care to think.

Essentially, leaders have to determine what their past has been like, what their present is like, and what their future should be like. This is because they not only want to be effective and inspiring leaders in the here and now but also endeavor to leave a legacy behind them long after they are gone. They want their name remembered years later in a positive light and as drivers of change. An example of this is the late Steve Jobs, who had a transformational approach as a leader. He wanted the world to be considerably different than when he found it in multiple areas, such as technology, entertainment, and communication. But his approach was not just to revolutionize those industries. He also wanted to change how people used technology, how people enjoyed entertainment, and how people communicated.

In the decades that he was the driving force behind Apple and Pixar, Jobs essentially reprogrammed people's approach to technology and how it could change their lives for the better. He also transformed how technology used to be, i.e., a colder, grayer, enterprise-style interface, to a user-friendly, colorful, and fun experience. That is his legacy: Being the person responsible for transforming people's lives around technology through his charisma, intelligence, and his understanding of what people wanted.

Like Jobs, your legacy will be all about the difference that you made. Managing and leading people is a crucial component; however, inspiring them to follow your lead and drive the transformation you want to achieve is going to leave a lasting impact. You can only make your people see your vision and goals the way you do by connecting with them, and for that to happen, you need to understand who you are at a human level and how you connect with others. This can be done by asking yourself questions to start thinking about yourself and your goals, which in turn leads to taking the necessary action to get closer to those goals.

Reflecting on who you are as a leader and a person also helps when you are faced with challenges or situations that put you under pressure. When you know how to deal with difficult situations, you don't have to spend too much time seeking counsel or figuring out a solution. Instead, knowing how you, as a leader, would handle such situations will provide you with a set of processes with which you can approach even the most challenging of situations from the get-go. Unless there are problems that do require the input of others, you should be able to tackle everything else all by yourself. But when you dither and take the wrong steps, which end up costing you, your position as a leader appears less and less stable to everyone around you. Your mistakes and failures can reduce and ultimately shatter your people's confidence in you.

One way to know yourself better is to create a hierarchy of goals. This approach was proposed by American psychologist Angela Duckworth, which emphasizes lower-level goals supporting greater goals one level above, and those goals supporting other greater goals another level above till they support the goal with the highest priority at the top. Each of these goals, when achieved, will lead to the greater goals being fulfilled till they lead to the goal with the highest priority. According to Duckworth (2016), the goal at the highest tier would be our life's philosophy which will guide how we live our lives and what we want to accomplish. This philosophy would be supported by the values or the middle-tier goals, which in turn would be supported by the various actions we take in our lower-level goals. Setting up our goals in this way helps us to understand the formula for success and identify any areas that are not working out so that they can be changed or adjusted.

There are also customized tools that help people understand their personality types as well as their strengths and weaknesses. Psychometric testing such as the Myers-Briggs Type Indicator (MBTI) and DiSC Personality Types help us understand our strengths and weaknesses, how we manage or communicate with people, what behaviors we normally exhibit, and much more. Though these tests can provide us with an interesting perspective into how we tick, keep in mind that most of these observations are our leanings rather than absolutes. Different situations will demand different personality traits or at least lean towards an opposite personality trait. For instance, leaders are extroverted most times but, depending on the situation, can choose to keep their viewpoints to themselves.

This also helps to create a leader's personal brand that others aspire to. Core values, philosophies, and goals become much easier to interpret when they are personified by highly talented and remarkable individuals. In sports, for instance, the philosophy and values of hard work, persistence, winning, and being the best can be reflected by the champions of the game, such as Michael Jordan, Roger Federer, Tiger Woods, Virat Kohli, Venus and Serena Williams, and many more. When young people are asked about what they aspire to be, they mostly answer about *who* they aspire to be, i.e., the next Michael Jordan or Steve Jobs. Creating a personal brand is the ultimate reflection of what a leader is all about and what they want to inspire others to be in one complete package.

Knowing yourself doesn't just have to do with the larger, overarching values and philosophies but also the smaller, day-to-day steps you take to realize those values and philosophies. Whether it is filing your tax returns, paying your mortgage, visiting the dentist, and so on, taking care of these day-to-day matters in a timely fashion clears your deck to take on the more complicated challenges. In the case of your professional commitments, always attempt to preempt upcoming concerns instead of putting them off at the last minute. This includes taking care of performance evaluations and promotions, finalizing budget allocations, releasing payments, and much more. Checking off your to-do list provides you more time for quiet introspection about yourself and the way things are in your organization so that you can think about further improvements and innovation.

As a leader, you should also embody the core principles, policies, vision, ethics, and procedures of your organization. This will help you to personify what your organization is all about and believe in its objectives. Unless you fully understand and espouse what your organization represents and hopes to achieve, you cannot expect everyone else to be invested in it. Leaders should essentially understand what goes on in an organization from top to bottom and how each piece of the puzzle fits. They should know what each department or team does, how their work connects with the work of others, and what would happen if they were not around.

Without micromanaging too much, leaders should also be the first ones through the door and the last ones to leave. This makes people realize how committed they are to the organization and what they should also aspire to if they take on leadership positions someday.

One way to learn more about yourself is to write down your thought processes on a day-to-day basis in a format that captures various details of your day and how they motivate you to understand yourself better. The next page shows a sample from Pantheria Media's *Life Log Journal*, which has a detailed checklist of how an individual's day can impact their perspectives for better or worse.

DATE ⬭ Ⓢ Ⓜ Ⓣ Ⓦ Ⓣ Ⓕ Ⓢ

THINGS I'M GRATEFUL FOR

1.
2.
3.

VITALS

WEIGHT	BLOOD PRESSURE	HEART RATE

TODAYS EVENTS

TODAY GOALS

☐ _____
☐ _____
☐ _____
☐ _____

TASK AND NOTES

TODAYS WINS

MY LOCATION

TODAYS LESSONS

MEAL

| Breakfast | | Lunch |
| Dinner | | Snack |

WATER INTAKE 🜄🜄🜄🜄🜄🜄🜄🜄 DAILY EXERCISE

TODAY I FEEL 😊 😌 😐 😠 ☹️

An example of the daily tasker/journal portion of the Pantheria Life Log.

The Importance of Self-Discipline

No matter how old you are or what stage of leadership you find yourself in, having self-awareness and self-control are the ideal ingredients for creating self-discipline. In the military, recruits are regularly drilled with both mental and physical reminders of who they are, what their purpose is, and how they can achieve it. A drill sergeant hammers these essential concepts every morning for hours. Even after cadets graduate, they continue to remind themselves of the same values with repeated practice and exercising discipline in every aspect of their lives. Self-discipline requires total dedication and holding yourself accountable whenever you stray from a goal. In personal cases, this could be when you promise to kick a bad habit by exercising self-discipline, but if you break the pattern, you will set yourself back and undo all your efforts. It gets worse if you do not realize that you have made a mistake and do not hold yourself accountable for it, which is why you should associate a reward and a punishment for every task in which you succeed or fail.

As a leader, you find yourself with a lot on your plate, and everything on it tries to get your attention. Even though you prioritize to the best of your abilities, there are times when certain tasks take precedence over tasks that you normally give higher importance to. These tasks include managing people, assigning responsibilities, evaluating performances, developing goals, resolving internal conflicts, solving problems, creating a positive atmosphere, and much more. But you are a leader because you possess greater intelligence and self-discipline to not be distracted from your objectives while also expertly handling or delegating any problems as you see fit. Nevertheless, there will be situations that call on you to divert your focus and energies toward them, but self-discipline can help you manage them more effectively. Through self-discipline, leaders ensure task success and keep an eye on the things that take precedence.

Self-discipline is the difference between leaders who keep a razor-sharp focus on their objectives and leaders who are easily distracted by the problem at hand. It gives them the right temperament to be dedicated to their goals while also leaving some space in their busy schedules to provide their input about a matter of great concern or a problem that their people cannot handle effectively. This shows that leaders don't just look at the big picture as a whole; they also see the tiny details that complete it. It highlights that leaders are ready to get into the thick of things, particularly when it also serves as an example for their people to follow. With self-discipline, leaders get to check off more goals every day and leave a lasting impression on their followers.

To understand how well leaders can implement self-discipline in their work and personalities, they should make a mental, or even a physical, checklist of different goals that they want to achieve each day. They should also take stock of their surroundings and find any areas that could lead to distractions or even tempt them to abandon whatever they are doing and focus on the distraction itself. If leaders are prone to making frequent visits to the break room, they can limit these by keeping food and drinks in their workspace. If they have a habit of checking their phone every five minutes, they should make it a point to lock it in their drawer before they start work.

A crucial aspect of developing self-discipline is accepting accountability. If you want to develop great habits that become the hallmark of your leadership, it is a good idea to get a mentor and hire a life coach. A mentor is a leader you look up to at work and who performs at a level you aspire to. Once they take you under their wing, they help keep you honest and in the loop on what is going on in the organization and how it affects your position as a leader. On the other hand, a life coach helps you develop skills privately that the organization or your leaders may want you to have but have no formal means of developing. A life coach (or business development coach) works for you and has no interest or incentive in prioritizing the needs of the organization like a mentor would.

Most leaders who are looking to improve their leadership skills may not have considered getting a life coach or are unable to due to other priorities or a lack of finance. Life coaches are high-performing individuals, and their time is valuable and expensive. Most life coaches have diversified into offering great content on the internet, such as on YouTube, especially for people who would like a taste of the experience. They have also published great learning material that can reinforce your commitment to developing self-discipline as well as other valuable concepts and skills in developing your unique leadership style. This book, as well as others on offer by the Pantheria Media Collection, can help you improve your understanding, but the personalized and tailor-made solutions that a life coach can provide you help break things down in ways that you can absorb. Life coaches also impart their own experiences for you to reflect on and also connect you with the right people who you can specifically benefit from.

Improve Your Self-Discipline

Based on Duckworth's approach of creating a hierarchy of goals, leaders should set their own goals on the lower tier that are realistic and contribute to the accomplishment of a larger goal at the upper level. This is a great way to exercise self-discipline as leaders can see the achievement of one goal leading to the next in a successful sequence that will help them accomplish bigger goals and stay highly motivated for doing so. It also helps if the goal itself interests leaders at a personal level, thereby easily holding their attention. Leaders also need to recognize the success of any goal, whether it is big or small, so that they continue with the same level of motivation and focus toward achieving the next one.

Exercising self-discipline is no different than exercising a muscle. It requires regular use and practice in order to improve. While some people may be fanatically devoted to self-discipline as an inherent personality trait, several others need to exercise it over and over again until they can reach a peak level of efficiency. Focusing on achieving your goals is only one important requirement which also requires the removal of distractions. Whether it is drawing the blinds around your office windows, putting your phone on silent, blocking any websites that hamper productivity, or even disabling your email notifications, you can always find out things that may, on the face of it, look like they are important but take your attention away from your priorities.

One way to eliminate these distractions is to recognize what kind of distractions take place in your day-to-day routine. For instance, note down what takes away your attention whenever you are busy with a task and at what time this happens. More often than not, some of these distractions are recursive and take place at a certain time, which makes it easier to identify and control. However, making a note of irregular and infrequent distractions helps you become more self-aware of how those distractions affect you and how they take away your focus. This way, you can avoid them the next time they pop up.

In case of any essential distractions, i.e., whenever another priority takes precedence, you should be able to have a solution available from your past experience or be able to delegate it to someone who can more actively take it up. This will leave you unencumbered to stay focused on your tasks at hand. Delegation is important as it will make sure that you do not take more on your plate than you can handle. Even though the temptation to take action yourself is going to be high, you should remember that there are more important matters that require your attention.

If nothing else, you can minimize the time you spend on each distraction by delegating the brunt of the work to others, such as gathering information about a problem, soliciting their feedback, and allowing them to take steps on their own. Not only will you be practicing effective self-discipline, but you will also be empowering your people to be more hands-on. This will also help them become better decision-makers as well as gain more confidence to solve problems on their own without approaching you in the future.

Having more time will also allow you to make considered and thorough decisions, particularly those on a larger scale. Leaders are exclusively responsible for several major decisions, such as assigning tasks, allocating resources, finalizing performance metrics, and so on. In any case, you must ensure that you have thought your decisions through while taking all factors into consideration. This may require taking more time, allowing leaders to consider the decision from all angles, but not too long that you become overwhelmed or drained once the decision is finalized.

You should also not be pressed into making a decision simply because you would rather be doing something else that has a higher priority. In this case, you risk making the wrong decision that can and will have serious repercussions afterward, which you will also need to deal with. When all these problems start taking up your attention, you also risk losing self-control which shatters your confidence and the self-discipline that you have spent so much time cultivating.

Meditation techniques have proven to play a crucial role in improving a leader's focus and concentration while also helping them center themselves so that they can see everything around them all at once. Mindfulness meditation, in particular, is becoming a go-to technique for leaders to understand what is going on around them at the present moment on a level playing field. It also allows leaders to keep a cool head and exercise sensibility over emotion whenever confronted with major distractions.

Mindfulness meditation emphasizes five basic steps: breathing, concentration, awareness of the present, letting go of stress, and meditating while walking. Even if you aren't confronted with any major issues, practicing mindfulness meditation on a daily basis can help you gain better self-control and reduce any tendency to make rash and impulsive decisions while at the same time keeping yourself focused on your goals and tasks at hand.

Similarly, it doesn't hurt to take a break right after any tasks or decisions that you know can leave you drained. As mentioned before, self-discipline is like a muscle that gets better with regular exercise, but overdoing it can add unnecessary strain on it. If you keep pushing on, you could find yourself tired, unmotivated, and even breaking down completely. While you practice self-discipline every day, you should focus on pushing yourself to an acceptable level each day and improve on it the next day; however, beware of pushing yourself to a higher level because it can prove to be too much.

Keep track of the tasks that tend to take a lot out of you and then schedule them as per your work schedule when you can take a break right after. For instance, leave a key and taxing job right before you head out for lunch while also allocating enough time to complete it. This way, not only do you feel a sense of accomplishment once you complete it, but you also reward yourself with a much-needed breather and possibly a hearty meal.

Benefits of Self-Discipline

Leaders with self-discipline possess an eye for detail and precision and also appreciate how effectively tasks are completed once they follow proper procedures. They also adhere strictly to their schedules for each task and the deadlines they set while also being prepared in case of any unexpected situations. Self-discipline is synonymous with order, structure, and control. It can be noticed in their surroundings, such as well-organized workspaces, clean and tidy desks, clearly laid out schedules in front of them, and strict adherence to the mantra "a place for everything, and everything in its place." They create a meticulous system by which they know exactly where something is so that they don't have to scramble to look for it when they need it, be it a file, a set of documents, a plan, or even items of stationery.

For someone on the outside, seeing someone this self-disciplined can appear to be obsessive and controlling. And while leaders who do exercise self-discipline may seem like they want to retain control over their feelings, decisions, and tasks, it also makes them more clear-minded about what they want to achieve, not to mention determined. They also recognize where others, i.e., their followers, might be losing their focus and leave themselves open to mistakes. This is where they can nudge them in the right direction and save them from any impending disaster.

Leaders with great self-discipline are also clear about their objectives through their communication and actions. Their example shows others what can be achieved by exercising self-control and prioritizing goals rather than acting impulsively and reacting to the first issue that grabs their attention. Self-discipline helps leaders keep their followers and groups fully informed about their objectives and vision, leaving no space for ambiguity.

As a final word on the subject, self-discipline is not just an integral part of becoming a great leader but also a great person overall. And while this book focuses more on developing skills and personality traits that serve you well in your leadership journey, you should also consider including self-discipline as a redeeming feature of your life as an adult overall. To help with this, one of my other books, titled *Super Basic Adulting*, is a great stepping point to gaining more in-depth knowledge and understanding about developing the foundations of your life as an adult, of which self-discipline is a major attribute.

CHAPTER

6

GROWING INTO YOUR LEADERSHIP ROLE

Leadership and learning are Indispensable to each other.
–John F. Kennedy

U nless you were born in a generational business or organizational framework that puts you in a pole position to be the next leader or a monarchy, chances are that your journey into your leadership role is going to be fraught with challenges and setbacks. But success and failure are both part and parcel of gaining the core knowledge of real leadership, which grows within you over time. Taking proactive steps is the way to go, but it is also essential that you take responsibility for both good and bad and distribute authority and influence to others. This will result in greater growth as a leader.

This chapter takes a two-pronged approach to how you can grow into the kind of leader that you are by owning up to your leadership style and authority type while at the same time looking for opportunities to offer an authoritative role to your followers for them to grow alongside you. At the same time, this chapter also focuses on how you can blend in your public and private lives to make them supportive of each other rather than two completely different worlds. This approach will greatly contribute to your evolution as a successful and fulfilled leader.

Own the Type of Leader That You Are

Having understood the various types of leadership and which one identifies with you the most, there will be a point at the beginning where you may disagree with that assessment. If you discover through psychometric testing or feedback from your mentor or coaches that you have an authoritarian style of leadership, you may vehemently oppose that notion and demand a different result. Ironically, that same demanding nature may actually be evidence of you having an authoritarian style.

But no leadership style is necessarily bad. Rather, these leadership styles work suitably well in the right environments and situations. Moreover, making allowances in your unique leadership style to incorporate traits from other styles helps you act with the best of all or most worlds. As a leader, you have to remember that your organization can benefit from more than one leadership style and authority type. This way, you can be the leader that corresponds perfectly with the goals and tasks in front of you without compromising who you are as a leader.

As mentioned above, assessing your leadership style and personality is the first crucial step to figuring out what makes you tick. This can be done from the earliest possible feedback you received at school when your teachers and fellow students described the kind of person you are. Your friends and family will also have first-hand experience dealing with you as a person, so they should be able to offer valid insights about your personality traits. From here, you can discover whether you are delegative or authoritarian, transactional or transformational, and so on.

This assessment doesn't have to apply only to your professional environment. It can also take into account how you act in personal settings, such as with family or friends. For instance, if you are among friends, are you the kind of person who takes charge? Do you set the tone with how you and your friends spend time together? In the same vein, do you lay out an agenda with how you and your family will be spending weekends or vacations? Or do you take input from everyone before making a final decision?

You should also factor in other critical aspects, such as whether or not you carefully consider your decisions or if you act impulsively when faced with a difficult situation. How you approach different situations, whether at home or at work, determines your preferences and how they all blend together to make your unique leadership style.

It is also important to recognize your values. People can tell a lot about a leader based on the values they hold dear. They can determine how a leader thinks, analyzes, and reacts in any given situation. They are default attributes that evolve over the years from childhood to adulthood and can become the defining feature of a leader's reputation. It is these values that inspire followers' trust, respect, and confidence in a leader and realize that they have their best interests at heart without any ulterior motive.

While it is important to lead by one's strengths, leaders must also understand the role weaknesses play in their leadership style. More often than not, leaders power through by relying on the areas that they are good at, but they overlook the areas where they need the most help. This can turn into a blind spot that may come to bite them when they least expect it. While fixing weaknesses isn't as straightforward as one expects, leaders can still aim to mitigate the negative effects of these weaknesses so that they do not interfere in their day-to-day roles. Showing a vulnerable side to your followers is not a sign of weakness. Rather, it shows how transparent you can be when it comes to admitting to these weaknesses, which in turn helps you to gain the respect and cooperation of your people. They will recognize that for all your talents, there are aspects of you that make you human, which is something they can always relate to.

This is where building a feedback-oriented culture in your workplace is a great boon. When leaders create a culture of open communication among people at all levels of the hierarchy, they are more likely to put forward constructive feedback. This feedback can come from peers, superiors, and followers and can provide insights into a leader's behavior, strengths, weaknesses, areas of improvement, personality traits, and values as they interpret them. Oftentimes leaders miss out on obvious areas of concern in themselves, and all it takes is to be highlighted by someone else to finally notice it. This feedback-oriented culture works both ways, as it also facilitates leaders to address any concerns they have with others. It improves communication between leaders and their teams and vice versa, which creates an atmosphere of openness and honesty with the intent of helping each other improve.

It also helps to take a look at the leaders who have influenced, mentored, and coached you over the years. Your journey as a leader has blossomed in no small part to the efforts of the leaders who have taken you under their wing. This includes parents, teachers, favorite uncles or aunts, sports coaches, supervisors, managers, and bosses. Whether consciously or unconsciously, you will have picked up on different habits, traits, perceptions, behaviors, temperaments, decision-making, and problem-solving abilities by viewing your own mentors and coaches. Even when confronted with a situation under pressure, you may have asked yourself what your mentor, former manager, or high school Ethics teacher would have done in the same situation. Before you know it, you will notice that over the years, you have cherry-picked the redeeming qualities of your mentors and leaders and added them to your own arsenal of leadership skills, hoping to emulate their success and behaviors in the way you do business.

Keep Your Public and Private Image Real

It is always "no rest for the weary" when it comes to people in leadership roles. They are always working mentally, if not literally or physically. Leaders don't stop thinking about how to innovate, how to delegate, how to reinvent, and how to perfect. But their existence isn't all about their role as a leader. Much like most public figures, leaders have an image that they portray for everyone in the world to see, but they also have one that they keep to themselves, such as their life and relationships with their family, friends, and close personal guides. Depending on how public a leader's life is, whether it is in a business or political landscape, there is always every chance that leaders will find themselves under the scrutiny of the public eye.

This applies to their life with people at work as well. Most employees automatically assume that their leaders live and breathe the organization, especially if they have ownership authority. It may even look like leaders are way too passionate about their organization, so much so that they make themselves available 24/7, whether in person or virtually. With such expectations, leaders may forget that they, much like everyone else in the organization, need to maintain a work-life balance and cultivate a separate self from their leadership self. Both these selves, i.e., their private and public lives, may mesh together at certain points, such as personality characteristics, habits, communication, and dedication. However, there should be clear lines drawn between the two so that leaders can have the best of both worlds and maintain their mental and physical health.

No matter what kind of leader you are, be it a small business owner with 10 to 20 employees or the CEO of a large multinational conglomerate, your time and energies will mostly gravitate toward your business and professional needs. Unlike employees or managers, dividing the time of day by spending 9-10 hours at work isn't a feasible option for leaders because they have to be present in more ways than one. In this case, leaders have to become flexible enough to balance the demands of professional and personal life.

For starters, it is important for leaders to understand that the concept of a public and private life doesn't apply to them. Instead, they have a life, period. This means that they treat both these lives as one giant tapestry that supports the other. It shouldn't be strange for leaders to talk about how much fun they have with their kids over the weekend and where they plan to travel soon. Similarly, they can also talk to their kids about things going on at work and make it sound interesting and fun. At times, leaders can even get their kids in on the action about how they would manage a certain situation at work and be surprised at the insights from someone with a different perspective. When leaders treat their lives as one, they don't have to worry about distinguishing between how they are at home and how they are at work.

It also helps leaders stay true to themselves. As long as they are able to keep the confidential and private aspects of their lives confidential and private, leaders can wholeheartedly embrace public scrutiny and showcase a lifestyle that is wholesome, fun, and down-to-earth. If, as a leader, you wish to keep your private life as open as possible, be sure to communicate with your family and loved ones about how they feel and how it might affect them. At the same time, you should also set boundaries among prying eyes as to how much of your private life is open for scrutiny.

Also, don't forget that there will be situations when you need to tilt the scales on which life gets more time and attention. There might be a situation at work that requires you to be there overnight or on the weekends, while an emergency at home will keep you away from work for some time. In both cases, make sure that you have adequate contingencies set up. If you are required at home, your team members should be able to operate without your presence and only contact you when your authority is required. If you are needed at work, your household should be able to cope without you for an extended period of time. Nevertheless, do not completely disconnect from either of them and check in periodically to ensure that all is well.

As stated earlier, you cannot do a 50-50 split between your public and private life. The buzzword here is "equilibrium" and how you can find yours. You may have to attend a call in the middle of your kid's school play, or you may have to forgo a meeting to attend your wife's art exhibition. But things have a way of balancing them out as long as you provide them as much attention as possible while not ignoring the other. One of the reasons leaders fail at maintaining equilibrium is because of taking undue stress, especially in critical situations. In such cases, they should always remain clear-headed and practice self-discipline to see how they can effectively manage their equilibrium.

Making mistakes is an inevitable consequence when you are not able to handle everything on your plate. However, these mistakes also offer an opportunity to evaluate what went wrong and how it can be avoided in the future. That is what growth in leadership and in general is all about. Observing how your commitment and drive to your business affects your life at home will give you fresh insights about how much time you should actually be devoting to it without alienating your family and friends. You will need your personal relationships to have your back when you need help as much as you will need your team. This support could come in the form of counsel, motivation, clarity, and reassurance, which can help you get through difficult situations without stressing out.

Your life as a leader is going to be a lot about give and take, or more appropriately, give and get in return. The more of your time and attention you give, the more you are going to get back from your peers, family, and friends. Leaders who are precise and well-organized shouldn't find it strange if they add lunch or a movie date with their spouse or partner to their planner. This goes to show how much they are allowing their private and public lives to mesh together. The key here is to be intentional about what you wish to do and keep things straightforward. The more the *public you* acknowledges the needs of the *private you*, and vice versa, the better they support each other.

Being tech-savvy with the newest innovations in managing your business allows you to be on the move and manage both lives at the same time. Whether it is taking your work with you on your family's weekend getaway to the Hamptons or being able to face-time your kids when they have a tricky math question for their homework, technology bridges the gap for you to easily manage both lives in close harmony. If taking a laptop everywhere is cumbersome, then using cloud storage services such as Apple iCloud, Google Drive, and so on can improve your mobility and make sure you don't miss a beat. Video conferencing applications such as Zoom, Google Meet, or Microsoft Teams are easily available on phones and tablets so that you can jump into a crucial meeting while you are away.

Above all else, be open and honest with your family about your role and responsibilities. Let them know what kind of things to expect in your life and how you can best handle them as a family. It also helps if you come together and create plans about what to do when situations call for you to give more time or give more virtual attention to work. Never be afraid to bounce your thoughts around with your spouse, partner, and kids, just to get a fresh perspective. This way, you keep your personal relationships with the people who matter positive and healthy, and they will want to contribute more and more to your success.

Additionally, remember to let your thoughts and reflections bleed out from time to time in a controlled and safe space, such as a journal entry. The next page shows a template where you can easily jot down whatever goes through your mind as you embark on giving your public and private image more meaning.

ADDITIONAL NOTES
(Thoughts, Reflections)

Additional Notes Page located in the Pantheria Life Log

Take Responsibility and Delegate

It's hard for leaders to let go, especially when it comes to something they have been accustomed to for a long time. There are several responsibilities that leaders enjoy doing and are very good at them. However, there comes a time when they should recognize whether or not handling those particular responsibilities personally is an effective use of their time. And by responsibilities we do mean responsibilities, not just tasks. Once leaders reach a higher level on the hierarchy, leaders understand that they should be handing over certain responsibilities to people below, but ultimately don't for one reason or another.

This can be problematic because these are the same responsibilities they were assigned when they reached a medium tier of leadership. Now that they have moved up, these responsibilities should be going to the new middle tier of leadership so that they can be groomed the same way the previous leaders were. Not doing so is an injustice to the newer leaders who are finding their place and developing the required leadership skills. They need to be following in the senior leaders' footsteps so that they can chart out the same path to success, but it won't help if the senior leaders hold on to those responsibilities.

There are a number of reasons why senior leaders hesitate to let go of such responsibilities. For one thing, leaders may not have been given similar responsibilities from their immediate superiors or were not trained on how to effectively delegate responsibilities to others. Due to this, they find it challenging to delegate responsibilities or even know what responsibilities to delegate and which ones to retain. Additionally, such leaders also miss out on delegating these responsibilities as learning opportunities for up-and-coming leadership due to fear of appearing incapable of handling those responsibilities themselves.

This can create an atmosphere in an organization where the growth of future leaders suffers, and they ultimately become resentful for not getting the same learning opportunities as their seniors. Therefore, leaders must identify the reasons why they refuse to let go of such responsibilities. Is it due to a sense of pride in having handled a responsibility so well for so long? Is it the fear of not expecting the same level of efficiency from the person they are delegating it to? Or is there a reason they doubt the abilities of the person next in line to handle it?

When faced with such a situation, leaders may feel apprehensive about the other person's ability to shoulder the responsibilities well or their own loss of control over something that they have left an indelible mark on. In either case, leaders feel melancholic about parting ways with these responsibilities, but they also have to realize that it isn't just a question of offering growth opportunities to the people next in line. It is also about their own professional growth and taking on newer, greater burdens themselves, and the only way they can do that is by freeing up their time and plate to take on more.

By understanding that delegating older responsibilities is as much a rite of passage as it is a stepping stone for themselves, leaders can start shifting their mindsets about how to delegate without too much risk. Firstly, they must assess who the best person for the job should be. There may be several likely candidates, most obviously who is capable of doing it. But aside from capability, leaders must also recognize who is most interested in such a responsibility as well as whose professional development it could help the most. Similarly, leaders can also gauge who among their team needs to take on more challenging assignments in order to get them out of their comfort zone. Knowing these reasons is important for leaders, especially when questions arise about why they selected who they did.

Secondly, leaders must also set expectations of the person they delegate to. They can set the day-to-day functions of these responsibilities as well as the performance metrics, the desired outcome, and its place in the greater vision of the organization. This will help to motivate the delegates as they will realize how important a responsibility is being put on their shoulder and what commitment is being asked of them. Furthermore, the leaders can set parameters about how much authority the delegate has while handling this responsibility and whether or not they would need to defer to them in certain situations. If the new person responsible is showing great signs of progress in handling the responsibility, the leader can then consider widening their berth to make more decisions on their own.

At the same time, leaders will also have to provide feedback on how the delegate is progressing on a frequent basis without making it look like they are micromanaging. Leaders can use these feedback sessions to find out how well the new person is doing in the role and what challenges they might be facing, not to mention if they have any ideas on how to make it more efficient and productive. If possible, they should make allowances for any initial mistakes so that the new delegates can learn from them and not end up getting demotivated. Leaders can also make arrangements for any resources or tools that the delegates require to take care of the responsibility, such as finances, additional staff, equipment, and so on.

Ultimately, leaders need to treat the transitioning of responsibility as an exercise in collaboration. They should be available just enough to motivate and assist their successors in making the responsibilities their own while at the same time assuring themselves that the responsibilities are in good hands. This will also lead to the development of a working culture where such transitions are performed according to set guidelines and as a matter of routine whenever required.

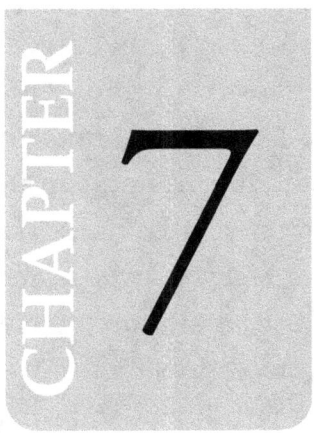

THE LIFE OF A YOUNG LEADER

Before you are a leader, success is all about growing yourself. When you become a leader, success is all about growing others. –Jack Welch

From a very young age, leadership skills can prove to be one of the best things that anyone can learn. These skills instill values and abilities that will help young people through their professional and personal lives. Whether through competitive sports, school projects, class assignments, volunteer work, and so on, leadership skills lay the groundwork for young people to develop a solid work ethic, reasoning, decision-making skills, organization skills, communication skills, and empathy. They learn how to manage difficult situations and how to come up with creative solutions, which builds up their mental and psychological development.

Young people also learn the much-needed quality of self-motivation that sees them through the majority of their professional careers. At the same time, young leaders greatly benefit from the evolving technological landscape, and its impact on the way business is done. This is especially true based on the strides technology has made in the last few decades thanks to faster and more efficient internet services bringing the world closer together, improved and dynamic portability through smartphones and smart devices like never before, and a completely new remote working ecosystem following the COVID-19 pandemic.

This chapter will focus on the importance of instilling leadership skills in our youth in order to give them a taste of handling authority as well as learning how to inspire and innovate among a group of like-minded individuals. It also helps young people understand that their need to become the face of a new change is a completely valid one that can be achieved through working hard and smart.

Importance of Leading When You're Young

By starting young, potential leaders can evaluate their own personalities and understand what unique qualities they have that are suited to leadership. From the outset, being a young leader can help them recognize their own abilities and know themselves a lot better than leaders who grow into leadership much later. Young leaders can chart out their academic and professional lives from the moment they can visualize what they want to do with their lives. This will enable them to map out what short and long-term goals they need to set, what skills they need to acquire, and what resources they need to utilize in order to progress further in their lives so that, by the time they graduate high school, they know exactly where they need to be heading. They can join professional development societies or clubs that facilitate their future potential. Aside from excelling academically, young leaders develop new skills and qualities that will help them realize their goals a lot more easily.

One very crucial skill that young people can learn is how to work in a team. Since childhood, young people are clustered into groups that are united towards a common goal. It could be a science project, a baseball game, or organizing the school fete. There are different ways that children can work together as a team. Teachers can assign complex puzzles, tasks, and problems that require students to communicate with each other and work out solutions. If set in a competitive environment, students can also understand the importance of working under pressure. Initiatives such as the Model United Nations, or the Model Parliament in some countries, is one such high-stakes program that puts young people in the thick of problematic situations where they have to put their heads together to come up with reasonable and effective solutions.

This brings up another critical skill that young people must develop in order to excel in their professional careers: communication. This could be related to interpersonal communication, presentation skills, and written communication. Students who understand how to listen and respond, as well as interpret the subtle nuances such as tone of voice, emotions, and other non-verbal cues, can become better communicators. They can also build much better relationships with their peers. Learning communication skills will help young people to express their opinions more clearly. Not only that, but they can also learn different cultural interpretations that their message can have. This way, they will be able to carefully consider their responses or statements to avoid ruffling any feathers.

Building teamwork and communication skills lead directly to learning how to plan and strategize in order to achieve a goal. Young leaders should be taught how to create detailed plans, implement them, and delegate them to different team members. This way, young leaders will also be able to learn the strengths and weaknesses of their team and understand who is better suited to perform a certain task. Young leaders will also be able to learn important negotiation skills that will help them. get the best out of their team, especially when it comes to assigning tasks that require them to put in long hours or make extra efforts.

Once young leaders start gaining more and more confidence in themselves and how they can lead others, they develop a sense of self-awareness a lot quicker than most other people in senior leadership capacities. From a very early age, having self-awareness about one's own skills and abilities helps people realize what sets them apart and what more they can do to improve themselves, be it skills, personal qualities, quirks, or behaviors. They can spend their professional career acquiring new skills and refining themselves as more capable and responsible leaders.

Furthermore, learning leadership skills when young will help them learn the power of inspiration and motivation. Once they start developing their own self-awareness and charting out their goals for their professional career, young leaders can then inspire others by sharing their own stories and setting an example about how they have dreamt about getting to that point in their lives. This ability to convince and inspire will develop more trust between young leaders and their followers and foster respect and empathy.

Because of their youthful optimism and positivity, young leaders possess a greater capacity for honesty, ethics, and integrity. During their period of self-reflection and how they have perceived the existing leadership model, young leaders would want to revolutionize what leadership is all about. A large portion of it will involve being more transparent and committed to empowering their groups and people. Young leaders will also understand how to solve complex problems independently and through teamwork.

There are other personality traits that should be imparted to young people during their formative years. This includes the ability to face tough challenges that will require them to take calculated risks. It should also prepare them not only for success but also for the possibility of failure, as well as instill in them a resilience that will help them bounce back from any such failures to learn from their mistakes and come back better than before. Young leaders should also learn how to curb their enthusiasm to the point where they do not act impulsively. While it is true that their passion is the main ingredient for their success, there are also times when being impulsive can lead to rash decisions without any forethought. This could likely be because young leaders may want to prove a point. Therefore, young leaders should also learn about the great virtue of patience and staying calm, particularly when faced with make-or-break opportunities.

Learning leadership skills at a young age also helps people to become more insightful as they listen to and observe different situations happening all around them, especially other people and their behaviors, body language, tone of voice, non-verbal cues, and so on. Observation allows young leaders to evaluate situations and analyze the best course of action of how to respond or proceed further.

Benefits of Young Leadership

At present, the US has around 66% of young leaders over the age of 40, 26% between the ages of 30 and 40, and 8% between the ages of 20 and 30 (Zippia, 2021). As even younger leaders start taking up more leadership roles while older ones retire or step back, the business landscape can see tremendous changes with regard to incorporating technology, resources, and revolutionary business practices. All these changes are aimed at enhancing productivity while at the same time taking an organization's welfare into consideration. The younger the leader, the better grasp they have on the needs of their people and the savvier they are on how to make things easier and better for them.

With the major advances in technology and resources throughout the 21st century, young people—Millennials and Generation Z in particular—have been much faster in picking up newer business practices and technology to refine their own business practices. Young entrepreneurs have relied on customized applications and software, such as communication tools, organizing tools, social media, and so on, to see them through to greater business success. This goes to show that young people and young leaders are more receptive to change than leaders who have been in their position for far too long. As technological developments have revolutionized businesses in one way or the other, young leaders have a far quicker uptake of these developments as they see their potential to enhance their organizations and achieve their goals a lot more quickly and more efficiently.

Because young leaders are highly passionate and more exuberant compared to the old guard of leadership, they do not hesitate to take risks, such as investing finances in acquiring new technology, upgrading existing business models to more secure, faster, and more efficient solutions, and getting these rolled out throughout the organization as quickly as possible. Taking such risks indeed has chances of failure; however, young leaders are nevertheless enthusiastic and highly optimistic about embracing these changes compared to the old guard.

Similarly, young leaders are never hesitant to share their enthusiasm and optimism with their employees and team members. Their passion and commitment to improving the organization and achieving its goals more efficiently see them motivating their employees with much more energy and positivity. On the other hand, the old guard mostly relies on restrained enthusiasm and carefully assessed directives. That isn't to say that organizations shouldn't carefully consider their options before plunging into new initiatives. However, with the rapidly growing and diversifying business landscape, organizations and their competition can better capitalize on opportunities that the old guard is likely to miss out on. This is why younger leaders can foresee what the future holds and how they are better able to realize it. Modern times call for modern methods to be implemented and adapted at all levels of the organization so that they are able to gain an edge over the competition.

Many young leaders believe in taking action immediately. This also includes providing feedback as and when needed to their team members about performance, achievements, improvements, and any shortcomings. On the other hand, older leaders prefer to have feedback delivered in more closed, private, and formal settings. In this scenario, leaders who take an active interest in delivering feedback in a more informal setting build better trust and motivate their team members a lot more efficiently simply by walking up to their desks and letting them know if there are any concerns or if they are doing well.

Employees who see young leaders giving feedback rapidly on the spot also believe that the leaders are taking an active interest in their personal and professional growth, which is more than welcome. As long as young leaders do not make it appear as if they are micromanaging and interfering with an employee's progress, they should be able to hand out appropriate and encouraging feedback which is constructive, helpful, and appreciative. Such feedback can be delivered as a sandwich of good, constructive, and good again so that leaders do not only focus on the negatives.

Because young leaders believe in achieving success and growth as early as possible, they will always be on the lookout for methods and processes that can get them results faster and more efficiently. If young leaders notice that certain procedures or processes are holding back an organization's growth, they will do their best to push forward improvements or even eliminate said processes. This can be seen as bucking tradition, where the old guard has gotten used to doing certain things a certain way. But organizations that stick to outdated procedures and processes risk becoming stagnant and being overtaken by the competition. These procedures and processes can be improved upon by recommending reform.

Challenges Faced by Young Leaders

One of the biggest concerns that young leaders face is the fact that they are young. In a sense, what that means is that they are still relatively inexperienced when it comes to actually leading. Because they have not been in a leadership position — or any other position — for very long, young leaders may not have the confidence they require to make major decisions more experienced and seasoned leaders would be able to make relatively easily. They may not be as decisive, they may have doubts about themselves or their judgment calls, and because of a lack of experience, they may feel that they have inadequate knowledge to make the right decisions about a host of situations.

Furthermore, young leaders are all about proving a point. They would like to have the faith that has been placed in them justified. But because of their self-doubts, they feel that asking for outside counsel or help may make them look unsuitable for the job. This can be a common concern in the initial stages of budding leaders. More often than not, young leaders tend to jump into the fray all by themselves without seeking out a mentor or a coach. The only judgment that they have to rely on is their own, not to mention the advice given to them by the managers that they are overseeing. In most cases, managers are cooperative and helpful; however, the final authority lies in the hands of a young leader whose indecisiveness and self-doubts will not be able to yield effective results.

Nevertheless, young leaders are required to step up to this position because they have the potential and the abilities to do so. They were not selected based on nepotism or preferential bias but because of their competency, skills, abilities, and insights. The first thing that young leaders will have to do in order to step up to the challenge is to recognize the fact that they are given a huge responsibility that they must live up to. However, it is not something that they are incapable of doing, no matter how they might feel or whatever doubts they might have. They are the ones who are in control. Instead of feeling inadequate and not up to the task, young leaders should do what they do best: plan, organize, and execute their goals and vision. Along the way, they should not hesitate to ask for counsel from their department heads as well as their mentors, coaches, peers, and any employees who they feel might be able to offer substantial feedback.

Secondly, youthful exuberance gives leaders the feeling that it is all about them and how they blaze their trail. To set an example, most young leaders want to make their mark on the business landscape whenever they are elevated to leadership positions. There are many barriers and records for them to break, whether it is the youngest entrepreneur under the age of 30 or the youngest billionaire in history. While there is nothing wrong with being ambitious, in fact, for young leaders, it is practically encouraged. However, it shouldn't make them lose sight of the fact that they have a larger responsibility to the organization and its vision, goals, and people. In their quest to make a mark, young leaders must remember that they are the representative face of the organization. The public recognizes the company's values, goals, and long-term intentions through the words and actions of its leader. Therefore, young leaders must be fully attuned to the goals of the organization to make sure that they are representative of what the organization is setting out to do. Their youthful exuberance and passion are better served at furthering the organization's agenda.

Ultimately, when it comes down to it, young leaders have to deliver results and meet expectations. This is essential when young leaders are heading important projects and assignments and juggling crucial deadlines. It can prove to be challenging, particularly when young leaders are working on a team of people who have had a far longer and wider experience than they have had in managing the affairs of the organization. It is also highly likely that most of the team members under the young leader's influence will be older, more seasoned, and would like to believe that they have a better understanding of the business than the leader themselves.

Building trust among such colleagues and team members can prove to be tricky, particularly when leaders want to be honest, open, and cooperative while at the same time not coming off as patronizing or condescending. After all, nobody likes a know-it-all. And organizations, particularly those that do not value diversity and inclusion by which younger people could have a much louder voice, won't be very receptive to new and fresh ideas. Young leaders must therefore set the tone from the start by proving that they are more than capable of handling critical assignments and tasks. They should also be able to show their presence as leaders and inspire their team members to get to the task at hand.

This can be done by setting goals and expectations not just for the team members but for themselves as well. They can start with small, manageable tasks for themselves in order to show their team members that they are ready to roll up their sleeves and work alongside them. However, this should not be the norm for leaders as they should be ready to delegate tasks far more frequently so that everyone on the team is performing at their best and also reporting to them as required. By setting a collaborative environment, young leaders can show their team members that they are reliable and serious about taking care of the projects and are more than willing to work together to ensure success.

Aside from respecting their team members as professionals, young leaders must also recognize them as human beings who require motivation, care, and consideration. For this, young leaders must be more empathetic to the needs of their team members so that they are better able to perform their tasks and achieve their goals. In their desire to make a mark at a very young age, young leaders show a great deal of passion, energy, and time to become the face of the organization. This may have them put in long hours because they are already starting to break down the barriers between their public and private lives. But that may not be the case for their team members, most of whom are family people and have their own priorities at home or elsewhere. Some of the team members may be pursuing an evening university course, others may be dealing with personal issues that may require psychiatric or therapeutic care, and some would just like to get home and spend some time with their children before they go to school the next morning.

Therefore, young leaders need to develop empathy at a very young age in order to better connect with their team members. This way, they can be more accommodating and provide them with the required resources to make their personal and professional lives a lot easier. Meeting up with team members and discussing any areas of concern or issues that they are facing will help leaders understand more about how far the extra mile they can go for their people. As a bonus, young leaders will also be able to earn the respect and loyalty of their people.

At the same time, these meetings can also be used to provide regular feedback about the team's performance. Empathetically connecting with people can help young leaders to offer constructive criticism easily because the team members can better trust their leaders once they have confided in them. Leaders can then kill two birds with one stone by offering them feedback as well as attempting to address their concerns. This will show team members that the leaders are genuinely interested in their concerns and are ready to help them as much as possible.

For young leaders to make the best of their passion and youthful enthusiasm, they should constantly be looking to improve themselves to become more leader-like. They should actively seek out coaching and mentorship opportunities from leaders whom they admire and take their own cues from as well as connect with other like-minded young leaders who are also looking for guidance. Such networking opportunities provide young leaders with different viewpoints and valuable recommendations from each other. Young leaders should also keep on their professional growth, as their time in the role is a constant learning experience. They should pick up new skills and refine their existing ones, such as communicating, listening, delegating, empathizing, and more. Learning can also be achieved through professional certifications and degrees that offer more in-depth knowledge that will enhance their leadership acumen.

Above all else, young leaders should always remember that they aren't perfect, no matter how passionate or savvy they are. After overcoming their self-doubts and gaining enough confidence, young leaders should be careful not to fall into the trap of over-estimating their potential while at the same time failing to recognize all the ingredients of their success, such as the support of their team and the insights of their role models. Young leaders must keep their egos in check and consider what is best for the organization rather than what will make them more recognizable.

8

IN THE LOOP
OF LEADERS

Communication among leaders makes everyone thrive or leads to everything falling apart. To leaders, communication means more than sending out emails or making grand announcements. It is a window into who they are as leaders and their qualities of authority, responsibility, entrepreneurship, trust-building, and empathy. By communicating effectively with their people, partners, and clients, leaders foster an aura of strength, optimism, and confidence. They should also use their communication to create a sense of welfare among their people so that they feel safe, appreciated, and motivated to deliver their best.

This chapter will look into the importance of communication in a leader's arsenal, whether it is through face-to-face or virtual interactions, writing, presentations, and general presence. It will focus on the three essential attributes of listening, reading, and communicating to show leaders how best to use their presence and abilities to get their message across.

Communication Among Leaders

No matter what a leader's message is, it has to sound genuine, sincere, and from the heart. For this, leaders are best advised to stay away from corporate-speak, buzzwords, or parroting official positions. Instead, leaders should find their own vocabulary and style that makes them appear as if the message is coming directly from them rather than a corporate directive. Leaders should always remember that their employees, teams, and followers do not appreciate being patronized; therefore, their message should be real and clear enough to be believed. It doesn't matter if they are able to deliver it as an eloquent speech or not; the message and the sincerity conveyed should inspire trust and confidence.

Moreover, leaders should always be open to listening first before speaking. Communication is a two-way street, and by listening to the other person, leaders show that they are receptive to feedback as well as another person's point of view. This, in turn, helps leaders to develop trust, transparency, and mutual respect. Also, by listening to their team and people, leaders are able to understand where they are coming from and what concerns they have, which will allow them to offer appropriate feedback and solutions. Listening without any interruption or prejudice to their people's opinions, feelings, ideas, and concerns shows that leaders are receptive and considerate and value what their people have to say. It also helps leaders to ask the right questions to gain further insights.

Once leaders show that they are ready to listen without prejudice, it will help people in the organization to speak up, especially if they feel apprehensive about airing their concerns or feelings directly to the leadership. If a leader can show that they are friendly, trustworthy, and firm believers in the value of their people to the organization, their people will want to do all they can to make their vision a reality no matter what level of the hierarchy they are at. Leaders must make their people feel safe at a psychological and emotional level so that they can feel free to offer their feedback and suggestions.

It is important to remember that communication isn't about what leaders say but what they do. It is true here that actions speak louder than words, but even if the leaders do not routinely show it, they should at least be seen to be present in front of their teams and people. Leaders should circulate among their people throughout the workplace to create the impression that they actively have their finger on the pulse of the organization. Only it shouldn't just be an impression; it is something that leaders should be doing by default. It will also allow leaders to receive on-the-spot feedback or for employees to raise any kind of issues that require the leaders' immediate attention.

The more leaders are seen to act and communicate with their team, the better their chances are to get their message across. Leaders are the glue that binds the organization together, so their presence is essential to keep everyone motivated, inspired, and dedicated to performing well. Frequent communication from leaders also reminds people of the organization's expectations, what values and traditions the organization holds dear, and what the organization hopes to see from each of them. Rather than using runaround terms such as corporate-speak, leaders should be clear, concise, and to the point. They can use statistics to supplement their information; however, piling it on and on will ultimately take away from the intent and meaning of the original message.

Also, it is not enough for leaders to simply convey information. If they want to show that it is coming from their heart, they must be able to relate it with personal anecdotes, stories, objectives, and goals that capture the imagination of their followers. Leaders should also visualize what they hope the message will achieve, which will, in turn, make the followers interpret the message a lot more vividly.

At the same time, leaders must also remember that their communication could raise plenty of concerns and questions. Therefore, they should remember what their people are like and what kind of questions they are likely to ask so that they can be better prepared to address those concerns without sounding too rehearsed. Leaders should also consider any blowback regarding proposals from their followers and have some alternative solutions present that may appeal to them.

Aside from verbal communication, leaders must also rely on non-verbal cues, body language, and facial expressions to convey their message. This will show that leaders are not reading out of a prepared statement and are genuinely making a statement right then and there. Maintaining eye contact and responding to questions and concerns with gestures, expressions, and so on helps them illustrate their position better and develop a good rapport with their audience.

Having a good understanding of nonverbal cues and expressions is also a great tool for leaders to notice any signs of disinterest, confusion, or opposition while communicating with their people. It could be anything from looks of concern to eyes popping out of their sockets, gasps of surprise, or even appearing bored, defensive, and uninterested in what the leader has to say.

Leaders are Readers, Communicators, and Listeners

One of the most tireless jobs a leader has is to ensure that everyone in an organization is on the same page vis-a-vis the goals, expectations, and overall vision. Whatever projects are being pursued, whatever ideas are being devised, whatever collaborations are being made, they all need to work towards making the organization's long-term future vision a reality sooner rather than later. To achieve this, leaders have to be both listeners and communicators as they keep the message consistent with their people at all levels of the hierarchy.

But in a survey by LinkedIn (Morgan, 2020), only 8% of around 14,000 employees worldwide who were asked about their leadership reported that their middle and senior-level leadership was effectively communicating the organization's goals and vision across the board to keep everyone on the same page. This is not very encouraging, especially considering how recent technological innovations have made it very easy for leaders to stay in close contact with their people, i.e., through instant messaging and workspace applications. At the same time, the traditional workplace is now making way for remote work at unprecedented levels as people from all around the world can work in any organization located in any country through the internet. The same goes for businesses expanding into new territories, offering solutions to clients from different backgrounds and ethnicities, and understanding the way business is done.

Therefore, leaders first need to identify the best channels through which they can spread their message across the board to every employee in the organization, regardless of where or how far away they are located. This is important considering that new digital communication methods are constantly evolving and will not even look the same in ten or even five years. Current virtual communications, such as video conferencing, are just a stepping stone to holographic communication that is becoming more real. Such methods will provide leaders with even greater visibility and let their followers interpret not just their words but their expressions, gestures, and hand gestures more intuitively than ever before.

One only has to look at the level of technological advancements with regard to communication over the course of the 20th and early 21st centuries to realize the scale of how communication channels have grown and adapted. Whether it is carrier pigeons from WWI to modern-day remote work communications tools such as Slack or Whatsapp Business, communication methods that are fast, robust, and constantly involving the people in the organization are seen as vital tools for continued success. Blackberry, a household name in the 2000s, launched its first email device with a revolutionary keyboard in 1999 to change how people sent and received emails. At the height of its success, major corporations around the world had issued Blackberry phones to all of their senior leadership and management, and heads of government kept Blackberry devices for its superior security.

One of the most memorable events involving Blackberry was during the crisis of 9/11 when the World Trade Centers in New York went down during a heinous terrorist attack on September 11, 2001. With several people trapped inside the rubble, it was revealed that Blackberry devices were still able to send and receive emails even though cellular phone services were disrupted. Many people were rescued after they were able to let others know of their possible location. In the midst of a crisis, all it took was a simple communication solution such as email to aid in disaster recovery.

This same evolution in communication technology kept businesses running in the wake of the worldwide COVID-19 pandemic. As businesses shut down their offices and people stayed at home following lockdown directives, remote workplace management solutions helped leaders keep things in order. It became far easier for leaders to manage remote teams by keeping in touch with them on a regular basis and creating an engagement platform for their employees that would let them interact with each other as they would in a regular office building.

Still, there is every possibility that no matter how advanced or robust communication technology becomes, a leader's involvement in using these tools is essential. Leaders who can create an effective level of participation with communication tools, particularly with remote management applications, can show their teams that they want to be kept in the loop while at the same time encouraging their teams to operate of their own volition. However, there is such a thing as being too flexible when it comes to letting remote teams operate on their own, so much so that leaders may find the teams going off on a completely different tangent.

One such example comes from Lighthouse Software, LLC, a Minnesota-based provider of mobile workforce management tools. On one occasion, their leadership was concerned when a remote team started performing below expectations. But once they started communicating with the remote team's manager, it emerged that the leadership had not been able to check up on the team for a few months. Because of this, the team had evolved into developing brand new goals for themselves that weren't in sync with the larger vision of the organization and leadership.

The above shows just how important it is for leaders to keep their people and teams in the loop, especially when teams are spread out across the world. Whether operating in different regions with offices, factories, stores, and so on or with remote teams deployed wherever feasible, a leader needs to remind people of the organization's purpose, vision, and goals so that there are no tangents or conflicting interests.

Apart from the medium of communication, leaders need to be open about sharing knowledge among their people as well as other leaders within the organization. Sharing important knowledge, especially proprietary knowledge and trade secrets, is a sensitive but unavoidable challenge in any organization. It requires excellent judgment, instinct, care, and quite a lot of legal documentation throughout the organizational hierarchy to ensure that sensitive information and knowledge are used only for the organization's benefit and never compromised. This could be one of the reasons that employees often find themselves dissatisfied with their workplace due to the lack of knowledge sharing by their immediate supervisors and senior leaders. This was observed in a study by Karl Sveiby in 2007, where nearly 3,000 employees in 12 companies were interviewed.

Nevertheless, leaders cannot expect to keep everyone in the organization on the same page without revealing important knowledge while also ensuring that there are safeguards in place to protect such knowledge . Once leaders foster an open and trusting environment, they lay the groundwork for ensuring such information's protection and proper use within the organization. This will help benefit people by increasing their level of knowledge about the organization, including the processes, latest developments, and feedback about a project or initiative. It will also encourage people to be more forward about making their own contributions, such as expertise, insights, and ideas, thus creating a melting pot of knowledge and information that leaders can channel toward the organization's success. Whether the ideas and knowledge shared by everyone are helpful or not, leaders can encourage an active discussion about the pros and cons of each idea to either pick the best one, refine others, and discard those that do not fit in.

Leaders should also remember to reward and appreciate the knowledge shared by their people so that they are motivated to make further contributions. When leaders treat their people's input respectfully and fairly, employees will acknowledge that their input has value. This will let them keep adding to the collective knowledge base of the organization and reduce the chances of people holding back. No one wants to sit on a good idea without ever revealing it just because they feel it won't be recognized or appreciated. Worst still, there is every possibility that people fear their ideas may be misappropriated and presented as someone else's, particularly by their immediate managers or supervisors.

This is where leaders should also ensure transparency of knowledge sharing. They need to assure their people that they can and should come forward with any kind of knowledge and information that can be used for the benefit of the team and the organization rather than for someone's personal gain. They can create open spaces for sharing important knowledge and ideas, such as town hall meetings, brainstorming sessions, corporate retreats, and even digital forums. This way, everyone knows where the information is coming from and who they need to thank and give credit for it.

In ensuring transparency and openness, leaders must not inadvertently put their reputations at risk. Working on your communication skills to encourage and motivate people is all well and good, but that doesn't mean you should be completely agreeable or flexible to every need that comes your way. It may also earn you the reputation of having a preferential bias where your decisions are not balanced. To prevent this, leaders need to remember what they are truly like, i.e., their knowledge of self, and identify when and where they need to get involved when it comes to communication. This includes situations such as conflicts, feedback, brainstorming, and more. They should make a note of how much their behaviors are either relaxed or confrontational by looking at the language they tend to use in such situations. They can also elicit this feedback from close colleagues, including other leaders, trusted team members, and lieutenants.

This will also help leaders avoid the common faux pas when it comes to being too open and honest to the point of compromising their position as well as other situations. This includes being too favorable to a certain position, point of view, or a person, not taking appropriate action in the face of conflicts, reacting in frustration due to failures in objectives, and risking their communication to become less effective and useful.

Encouraging Healthy Conflict

As a rule, leaders should encourage collaboration and brainstorming as part of a healthy and communicative work environment. But in their desire to create such a space, leaders have to keep in mind that not every idea their team or people throw at them is going to be the next big thing. In a sea of ideas, you will find some rare gems that, when fully developed and refined, can change the landscape for the better. But along the way, there are going to be several bad ideas that need to be recognized for what they are and then filtered out. For every Mustang, there is a Pinto; for every iPod, there is a Zune; for every Game Boy, there is a Virtual Boy. Organizations and their leadership should be able to distinguish between which ideas will be gold and which will be lemons.

This is only possible when leaders also enable a concept in communication called healthy conflict. It is where various parties can engage in an exchange of ideas while also keeping room to debate the pros and cons of the ideas. This needs to be done with the understanding that no matter what the drawbacks of any bad ideas are, they can be critiqued and hashed out in an environment of mutual respect, understanding, and trust. When leaders keep themselves approachable and actively listen to their people without fear of prejudice, they enable their people to operate under the mantra that no idea is a bad idea. That isn't necessarily a bad thing, as it helps leaders teach their people the importance of innovating and refining their ideas to the point that they suit the organization's vision completely. But when leaders forget to say no to bad ideas just because they do not want to create the impression that they do not value their employees, it is a very risky proposition.

It also works the other way around, where employees are programmed to become yes-people and agree by default to everything their leadership says, even if it has the potential to be a disaster for the organization. An environment of healthy conflict is essential as it is a place where both leaders and their followers can respectfully disagree over different matters, whether it is over major product innovations or deciding which brand of handwash liquid to use in the office restrooms.

There is an art to disagreements that requires patience, care, and empathy. Any areas that a person disagrees with can create an upsurge in their emotional state where they react to get their dissent across. This shows that people are so heavily invested in something that if someone suggests a bad idea, they lose control of their feelings when responding. All it takes is a change in a leader's tone of voice, facial expressions, and body language to see that they are being forceful about their disagreement. Unfortunately, this can be misconstrued as an overreaction which can shut down any opportunity for healthy conflict and instead result in feelings being hurt and morale going down.

Evidence of how avoiding disagreements has been changing the way people think and react to new information is all around us, with phenomena such as the "cancel culture," labeling anything as "fake news," and spewing hate-filled comments at anyone who provides a dissenting opinion becoming the norm. In such an environment, employees are right to be concerned about how their opinions and disagreements will be handled, especially in an authoritarian leadership. No one wants to risk losing their job or, even worse, being ostracized by everyone else as a troublemaker.

Therefore, leaders are responsible for making room for an environment where healthy, respectful, and constructive disagreements are provided as and when necessary to provide contrary views not just for the sake of it but for providing the other side of the coin. Any creative idea or solution that appears to be a no-brainer must be evaluated for all the pros and cons in order to avoid a potential failure. Furthermore, leaders must also remind everyone and themselves that expressing disagreements is well within everyone's right to free speech. Any person utilizing this right cannot be persecuted directly or indirectly, i.e., termination, demotion, unfavorable performance reviews, discrimination, etc.

To achieve an environment of healthy discourse and exchange of ideas, leaders must welcome both conventional and unconventional ideas and encourage people to air their apprehensions as they see them. They should not deliberately try to avoid conflict and instead allow opposing viewpoints, especially in a culture that has not been tolerant of views before. Leaders must therefore use their discretion on how to elicit honest opinions that are carefully considered and come from genuine concern about any idea's appeal or problems.

One way to make healthy conflict the norm is to open the floor for airing concerns at different stages of a project, such as the initial kick-off meeting, the proposal stage, the quality testing, and the execution. Employees can then let leaders know about any immediate concerns, which will help leaders either put their minds at ease or take their opinions into consideration. This will also get employees used to the idea that their opinions, even contrary ones, are welcome and valued.

The key here is listening. In every stage of a project or an idea, leaders should continue to listen even after a direction has been finalized. They should take in opinions from all quarters, including the stakeholders, teams, and people responsible for the execution. They should also listen to any new information that comes along the way so that they can continue fine-tuning any ideas as required. Furthermore, leaders should be flexible with certain projects and strategies where there is always room for change and improvement, depending on the feedback they are getting from their team. Their initial strategies can be educated guesses or hunches about which way they should be going unless something better comes along.

Simultaneously, leaders should try not to jump the gun when they see an idea going wrong. There will be points when things do not go as planned, and the first instinct will be to pull the plug on the entire project. However, there are other factors to be considered, and if leaders and their followers have foreseen any upcoming changes, they should then stay the course. They should also challenge themselves to see things through after reevaluating the situation so that they can make a breakthrough rather than completely losing faith.

Most importantly, leaders must remember that healthy conflict is necessary to create a challenging and dynamic working environment and promote diversity and inclusion. This way, they will be able to welcome new ideas and solutions. Nevertheless, healthy conflicts are not in any way supposed to be taken personally, nor should they be reciprocated in the same manner. It could result in a conflict escalating to an offensive tone, such as racial or gender-based discrimination and penalization.

Communicating with leaders is a highly dynamic proposition with its own set of challenges to maintain equilibrium between them and their people. Leaders must therefore be more magnanimous and accommodating to diverging opinions so that their teams become stronger and more productive.

IMPORTANCE OF FAMILY
AND COMMUNITY

One of the most important ingredients of being a great leader is to have excellent relationships with the local communities. This can be achieved by caring for the community's interests and promoting better cooperation through teamwork. Leaders who are interested in making changes at the grassroots level will start by looking for initiatives that can be accomplished within their own communities first. If they wish to become a guiding force for the improvement of their own communities, they should maintain healthy relationships with community leaders and all the relevant stakeholders.

Leaders who have excellent communication skills and know how to build trust and influence among their teams should have no problems doing the same in building their relationships with community members. It requires the same practices of speaking, listening, and communicating with the communities while also appealing to their interests, values, beliefs, and social circumstances.

This chapter helps leaders to understand how they can become even greater at leadership by building relationships with communities and their people at the grassroots level.

Focusing on Grassroots Leadership

In the wake of the COVID-19 pandemic, people all around the world have begun to re-evaluate their purpose in life, especially as it pertains to their role as employees and workers working a daily grind to achieve a livable wage. As workplaces shuttered their doors for most employees while others started working remotely from the comfort of their homes, people started asking themselves whether all the hard work they put in over the course of their lives was even worth it. Because people no longer got into their cars or on the subway to make an hour-long commute to work while rushing through an unhealthy breakfast to work behind a desk or operate heavy machinery for the remainder of the day till they could get to see their families after dusk, they started to question if making all this effort, spending all this time, and giving all their creativity was actually enriching their lives at all.

Being taken out of the workplace gave people the time to reflect upon themselves as individuals and human beings, and they realized that, in most cases, their essential needs were not being fulfilled. At home and away from the demanding rigors of the workplace, they found themselves with a brand new sense of spiritual contentment and fulfillment. This notion was further amplified through the Internet as people started posting pictures, videos, podcasts, and other content about how they have gotten to connect with themselves, their families, friends, and nature after being shut out of their day-to-day grind.

This phenomenon has not gone unnoticed by leaders as the impact of the workplace being left vacant in the wake of the lockdown restrictions became more apparent. Leaders realized that the new normal that came into effect right after the pandemic put people in their homes, i.e., working from home on projects with minimum supervision and maximum flexibility to get the job done as long as it was getting done on time and efficiently, their workforce can be just as productive without being in the physical confines of the workplace as they had been while they were in it. Giving their people the option to work in the comfort of their own homes where they could focus on living a healthy, balanced, and enriching lifestyle with their family and loved ones shows that employees can be trusted to deliver productivity and efficiency without the need for being managed to the nth degree. A study by Stanford University reported that work productivity had increased by 13% by working from home. This could be attributed to a quieter workspace as well as flexibility in working hours, not to mention the amount of time and energy reduced by not having to commute to work and being able to set one's own schedule. The study also observed that worker attrition had decreased by 50%, a significant indicator of overall employee satisfaction (Bloom et al., 2015).

This radical shift in the employees' priorities, perspectives, behaviors, and attitudes is recognized by leaders as fundamental to how they perceive working in the next few decades. Leaders understand that their followers and team members are looking for more than just professional growth at work; instead, they are also seeking out their true purpose. One way leaders can facilitate this is to organize community service programs that are focused on helping people discover their purpose and bring about societal change. That, in turn, can help leaders develop a greater organizational culture by engaging with diverse communities across the board and encouraging more inclusion by offering working spaces and conditions that facilitate people to work the way they feel comfortable.

Focusing on such levels of grassroots leadership helps leaders to provide employees with fulfillment, seek out their true passions, and encourage and motivate them to offer new ideas, perspectives, and innovations. Leaders should harness their people's viewpoints about what they feel an ideal world should look like, which is one of the main precepts of going into leadership in the first place, i.e., to bring about a sea change. Not only does this ignite valuable conversations and debates about what can be done to make the world a better place, but it also enhances engagement and dialogue so that people feel comfortable and confident in talking about the things that matter to them the most.

Grassroots leadership focuses on embracing the values and beliefs that employees and workers have in order to build a more inclusive and welcoming culture. Once employees are given the opportunity to be heard, they will then be more than willing to give back to the business community. This could be seen in forms such as ideas and innovation, as well as developing the spirit of teamwork, friendship, camaraderie, and unity. Focusing on grassroots leadership helps to engage people with each other and work together as a team to achieve a common goal and bring societal change. These will be efforts that people can be genuinely proud of, especially by understanding what impact they have on their own communities and their future.

With better team bonding and unity, leaders can help them discover a sense of purpose that they previously did not have. It provides employees with spiritual fulfillment, contentment, and a sense of pride over having done something that has lasting value and meaning not just to themselves but to the community at large. Once employees feel proud of their work, they will be more than willing to stay on and continue the waves of change by devising new methods and opportunities where they can create a meaningful and lasting difference.

When employees see that their efforts are being rewarded, they will not feel the need to consider leaving such an organization or leadership. Moreover, they will continue to motivate the next generation of people to become a part of the cause and actively contribute towards such grassroots leadership programs, eventually leading them to a career path in the same organizations. Also, doing something that people love will help them feel a lot better about what they are doing and not stress about whether or not they are doing things well. Focusing on community programs naturally allows people to have a positive and optimistic attitude. This is also important to create a healthy work-life balance where people feel that their efforts are not just a professional endeavor but also a personally enriching one.

Facilitating Community Service

To facilitate greater community leadership, leaders must correctly understand the practices, perspectives, and values of a particular community in order to contribute towards it in a productive and positive manner. The only difference is that instead of a team of loyal employees who are naturally inclined to helping the leaders achieve their vision, community leaders will have a team of local volunteers who are also invested in improving their community and must exercise influence over the leader themselves. There are other participants, including government authorities and businesses, looking for opportunities to deliver corporate social responsibility.

Nevertheless, leaders are responsible for managing, planning, and executing certain programs and initiatives that are aimed at enhancing the welfare of the community in general.

The most obvious area where community leaders can make an impact is by improving the physical infrastructure of the location of the set community. This usually involves taking care of maintenance, construction, renovation, and upkeep of various public places and facilities. This includes roads, community centers, parks, libraries, schools, hospitals, and so on. Oftentimes, local governments and state authorities either neglect or are not adequately funded to maintain these key amenities that a community needs. This is where businesses can step in to utilize their experience in mobilizing people to deliver better and more visible results; while also cooperating with local and state authorities so that their efforts are within the confines of the law.

As an example, this has been put into practice by the Lawrence Community Works (LCW), a nonprofit organization dedicated to the social and economic upheaval of Lawrence, MA. The nonprofit aims to create opportunities for the residents to have a say in the town's economy, infrastructure, and active leadership. This is achieved by organizing community gatherings, hosting speaking engagements, organizing dinners, and renovating public spaces such as a community recreation center. The organization has enabled thousands of residents to come together and take on the responsibility of leading the town of Lawrence toward revitalization and prosperity.

Community leaders have a personal motivation to take on the mantle of responsibility for making sure that their communities are prosperous, well-equipped, stable, and safe. As community leaders are not elected, they can volunteer to put in their time, efforts, and resources, usually with the backing of their own business interests. At the same time, community leaders must agree to the terms and conditions set by the local and state authorities and law enforcement agencies to ensure that they comply with appropriate regulations and do not unfairly benefit or profit from these community outreach efforts.

All it takes for people to decide that they want to be community leaders is that they want to make a valuable addition to their community's welfare and prosperity. Since a community leader does not need to be elected, they can simply make it known that they are going to be looking out for the welfare of the community. Unlike traditional businesses, community leadership doesn't have the same kind of performance metrics. Instead of sales targets, profitability, expansion, and growth, community leaders focus on delivering a great living experience for the people. Successful community leadership helps to empower communities by providing knowledge, skills, and resources to improve their standard of living as well as partnerships with businesses to provide facilities such as employment, economic growth, experience, and other benefits. This way, community leaders can empower their people to bring about active social change.

Community leaders can set individual goals that slowly but steadily improve the community's standing. By encouraging volunteer work and a sense of responsibility, leaders can create the drivers for the community's uplift. This will require them to appeal to the people and their feelings about how they wish to see this community in the long run and what they can do to take care of the various problems that are plaguing them.

There are several examples of community leaders using their skills, expertise, and resources to make their immediate communities a better place. For instance, a nonprofit called "Blacks In Nonprofits" aims to bring nonprofits in the Black community worldwide to come together and exchange resources, ideas, and expertise to facilitate their individual causes. Led by Dr. Rho Thomas, the platform has swelled to number around 25,000 nonprofit leaders in the Black community so that they can come together and devise new strategies to serve their immediate communities better.

Similarly, a volunteer group-turned-nonprofit called "Mama Dragons" has taken up the cause of helping and empowering mothers of LGBTQ+ children. It has been doing so since 2013 with a membership base of over 7,500 to help spread awareness of affirming practices for mothers to better connect with LGBTQ+ children in order to help them through their life choices and keep them safe from the threats of depression, self-harm, and suicidal tendencies.

Ingredients of Successful Community Leadership

Community leaders will be working a great deal with volunteers. Much like leading a team of professionals in business, community leaders can use their exceptional skills to mobilize people to achieve a common goal—it isn't that different from community leadership. The only difference is that leaders have limited options to choose from when it comes to community volunteers. In the traditional working environment, leaders can recruit individuals based on their abilities, motivation, and commitment. On the other hand, community leaders will have volunteers who are well-intentioned and ready to do their part to uplift their community.

While that in itself is a noble cause—it also happens to be the cause of the leaders themselves when they chose to get into community leadership—it does leave leaders in a pickle that they do not have greater control over the kind of volunteers that they get to recruit. Working to uplift the community requires both physical and mental fortitude, and volunteers will be a very odd mix of the two. Some of them will be very skilled at taking care of physical chores such as doing renovation work, cleanups, and the like, while others may be more adept at offering knowledge-based contributions such as teaching underprivileged children, offering counseling and therapy sessions, and so on.

It shouldn't be very difficult for community leaders to assess the individual skills, personal qualities, talents, and experiences that they are willing to bring to the table so that they can channel these resources toward appropriate uses. At the same time, leaders must also realize that the volunteers are coming in with the best intentions and that their contributions should be valued for what they are rather than be frowned upon for what they aren't. This will help maintain motivation levels among volunteers as well as others who can walk in the volunteers' footsteps to do their part for the community.

Secondly, leaders must also acknowledge that their volunteers will have certain needs in order to get the job done. Aside from the required resources that will help the community uplift project, the volunteers themselves will have different habits and approaches that must be carefully considered before assigning certain tasks. For instance, a person assigned to take care of building fences for a park may have a conflicting approach with some other volunteers who favor a different style of laying a fence. Community volunteers more than likely know each other from years of living together, and there may be certain preferences or animosity that can impede uplift projects. Therefore, community leaders must recognize the different behaviors, relationships, and approaches their volunteers can have to appropriately influence them toward achieving their goals.

This is also going to be important when leaders need to count on their volunteers to work together as a team and where the lessons of building trust and leveraging it for influence help community leaders to become more visible in the uplift programs. They will also be able to help people feel that they can approach the leaders to obtain the necessary resources and assistance to meet those goals. It will also allow leaders to use their communication skills to impart their vision and philosophy toward what they can do for the community while also taking necessary feedback and encouraging healthy debate among the volunteers and the residents towards setting their objectives. As a result, community leaders create stronger and lasting relationships among the volunteers and the residents that will continue to grow even after the community uplift projects have been completed.

Though dedicating time and energy towards community service is welcomed and appreciated, leaders need to show that they are doing this for genuine and altruistic reasons rather than capitalizing on a public relations opportunity. The only way leaders can show genuine concern for the community is by rolling up their sleeves and pitching in to lead by example. This way, volunteers and the community at large can recognize their efforts and be doubly motivated to do the same. Aside from that, leaders should also establish channels of communication with the volunteers and the community so that they can gain valuable feedback about the changes that they have gone about and how they can continue to make the community a great and safe place to live.

Leaders should also be open to criticism if any of their steps do not reflect the inherent values of the community. They should be ready to address any questions or concerns that community members may have about their goals and intentions. Community leaders need to take the people on board before they implement major decisions that could have lasting effects on the way these people live.

It isn't enough for leaders to focus on the community uplift schemes in the here and now. They also need to think about the future and how the communities can be developed in the years to come. The most important way they can do this is by focusing their attention on their volunteers by empowering them to make decisions on their own and institute changes. Leaders will have a great opportunity to mentor the future generation of leaders in the form of their volunteers so that they can learn the values of self-discipline, motivation, responsibility, and building trust.

LEADERS PREPARE LEADERS

A good coach can change a game; a great coach can change a life. –John Wooden

L eaders providing constant feedback is one thing, but using the methods of coaching and encouragement to improve their people's lives, motivation, and performance is a completely different ballgame. Like a sports team, leaders want to assemble the best of the best and the brightest of the brightest; however, there will also be times when they recognize the potential of someone hidden deep underneath. If leaders recognize this potential and firmly believe that it can be brought out, all it takes is for the leader to chisel away the imperfections and carve out their final form.

More importantly, followers will also respond to their leaders' efforts if they believe that these efforts are borne out of genuine faith in them. Once followers see that their leaders are equally invested in people who are already shining bright and the ones who still need to find their footing, leaders will earn their loyalty as they understand how important it is to get under their wing. Through the right kind of coaching and encouragement, leaders can help their people rise to the level that they are meant to be at, however, leaders must be careful to keep their coaching techniques constructive, unbiased, and unprejudiced in order to succeed.

This chapter will help you understand how coaching and encouragement can be used as a tool to help your people who are either struggling with the basics of a task or job or have yet to start working at the standards that you expect them to. It will also show you that while some people may seem like they can't learn, it is only because they have A) never had anyone believe in them for various reasons, B) they are overwhelmed with the tasks, or C) they need further and clearer instructions and training on how. This is where you also get to learn about an as-yet undiscussed type of leadership style: coaching leadership.

Understanding Coaching Leadership

As a leader who is still looking to gain the right kind of insights and confidence on how to lead better, coaching leadership is a surefire method to boost not just the confidence levels of your people but also of yourself as a leader. The principles of training in the Navy emphasize a "sink or swim" approach. The way it works is this: Those who can swim are assigned more laps in the pool, whereas those who sink are relegated to the kiddie pool to learn how not to sink. As a result, the trainees who were able to swim were assigned more work while the "sinkers" were put aside to keep improving till they could join their fellow swimmers to shoulder their burden. This would require coaching them until they get the hang of the basics and get on equal footing with the rest so that they are ready to take on the challenges that lie ahead.

This is how coaching leadership essentially works. As part of the Situational Leadership model developed by behavioral scientist Paul Hersey and author/business consultant Ken Blanchard in the 1960s — also known as the Hersey-Blanchard model — coaching leadership highlights the value of offering guidance to people who are highly motivated but lack direction. This style helps leaders identify their team's strengths, weaknesses, skills, and motivation to help them improve through learning and practice. Most modern organizations rely on coaching leadership to develop their employees and their skills. This style also helps to develop a learning culture that offers opportunities for increasing professional knowledge, skills, and expertise under the guidance of an experienced mentor.

Leaders can start implementing coaching techniques in their own leadership style by evaluating the teams thoroughly. This includes their habits, approaches, motivation, and present productivity levels in order to have a baseline from where to start. Once this evaluation is complete, leaders should formulate a plan through which they can fill in the gaps in their people's knowledge and abilities. One way to gauge where your teams lie is to simply ask them one by one. Interviewing your team members to get to know them better will help you to make a note of all their personal qualities, habits, and unique quirks. At the same time, asking open-ended questions can offer greater insights into how they feel about their present situation, how much they want to learn to be better, what they feel they need to improve, and so on.

As these interviews will be conducted one-on-one, leaders can utilize this opportunity to provide valuable feedback based on the answers they have received as well as their observations. Using the sandwich approach for feedback, leaders can focus on their followers' strengths first, followed by the areas that need work, and then topped off again with another dose of praise. This helps leaders to soften the blow and also for followers to realize that their leaders aren't only focused on pointing out mistakes. Once leaders offer their praise and critiques along with how to rectify any issues, their team members become more inclined to want to learn how to improve and maintain their positive attributes.

Next, leaders should take some time to reflect on the information they get from their followers as well as the feedback they provide. This will help leaders gauge how their coaching efforts are able to make a difference or if they also require improvements. This can be observed from the followers' responses to their suggestions, i.e., whether or not they agreed with the leader's assessments and the proposed methods and techniques to improve themselves. At the same time, leaders will find it helpful to make a note of unique feedback suggestions so that they can use them for any similar future cases while also noting down the different problems that come their way. This will allow them to come up with common best practices that can be used by other leaders for their own coaching endeavors.

Coaching offers leaders the opportunity to develop better trust and rapport with their teams. People are less likely to listen to and act upon any given advice if they do not feel they can trust their leaders to look out for their best interests. This may be due to prior negative experiences with others or even the same leaders in which they found themselves regretting the trust they put in. In the case of the latter, there is every possibility that leaders may have learned from their mistakes in the past and are trying to turn over a new leaf. They can try to rebuild the trust by admitting their previous mistake and offering a genuine and heartfelt apology and a commitment to make amends. This will help leaders appeal to the said followers and hope to repair the broken trust so that they can offer their feedback. Similarly, followers may not want to listen to a leader's feedback if they do not feel respected or appreciated by them. This is where the praise-critique-praise can offset such feelings and reduce any hesitation or apprehension in the followers.

Providing feedback and encouragement to improve isn't going to be enough. Leaders must remember that coaching is an ongoing process that should be evaluated for its effectiveness. The best way to do this is to follow up with the people they have coached to see how they are performing and feeling after the feedback. This can be done through scheduled follow-up meetings or a casual conversation at their work desk in order to gauge the feedback's effectiveness. It will also help leaders hold themselves accountable so that they realize whether or not their coaching methods are achieving the results they had intended while also keeping their people on their toes so that they don't forget to put the training and correction they have received into practice.

It also helps if leaders actively seek advice from their mentors or fellow leaders on how to provide effective coaching and encouragement or get themselves coached on how to coach others well. No method works to 100% effectiveness in every situation, so leaders must make sure that they are themselves coachable. They can ask questions from their mentors or fellow leaders or find resources such as books, articles, and online training sessions that will help them become better at coaching. An exchange of information among like-minded peers and leaders will vastly improve their coaching skills as they come across different and potentially more effective coaching methods.

Pros and Cons of Coaching Leadership

There are many benefits to coaching leadership. For one thing, it facilitates leaders to be present a lot more than they may have been previously, thus providing continuous and visible leadership to the team as long as it doesn't spill over into micromanagement. It also creates a positive working atmosphere and a drive to do better. When employees see that their leadership is taking an active interest in their performance through coaching and encouragement, they will want to be at their best while also making sure that they aren't afraid of being watched.

Aside from enhanced productivity and performance, coaching leadership also helps improve communication between leaders and their people. It encourages freedom of sharing opinions that will mutually benefit both parties by helping them to discover where each of their strengths and weaknesses lies. Leaders who effectively coach their followers not only help them to work out their areas of improvement but also gauge how well they perform as leaders and coaches in order to either maintain or reorient themselves as necessary.

Leaders also gain a deeper understanding of what it means to be a coach and a trainer. They learn more about auditory learners, i.e., those who need verbal explanations in the form of conversations and discussions to understand tasks. At the same time, they understand how to coach people who are visual learners, i.e., those who learn by reading or looking at visual aids such as pictures, videos, charts, maps, graphs, and so on. If that weren't enough, leaders also get to experience what it is like to help kinesthetic or haptic learners, i.e., those who must physically perform a task to learn how to do it or get better at it, preferably with an experienced person to guide them.

As leaders do not necessarily have an educator's background, coaching offers them a unique opportunity to develop their teaching skills that can help all three of the above learning styles, i.e., visual, auditory, and kinesthetic. Leaders discover that there is more than one way to help their people get better, particularly if there is a different learning style that helps them process information faster and more efficiently. Understanding the different ways leaders can address the learning needs of their people is an integral part of their leadership journey, but oftentimes it is not heavily focused on in lieu of developing an organization's vision and strategy. However, coaching is also an investment that organizations make in their people, which is an investment being made in the organization's growth.

Moreover, coaching also helps leaders to reevaluate how they treat their people in terms of professional and personal growth and efficiency. By employing different coaching methods, leaders get insights into the effects of these methods and what is best to use with a certain kind of team member. It also lets leaders solicit feedback from their team about how well their coaching and encouragement methods are doing. This feedback can be collected anonymously to increase participation as well as the possibility of getting honest answers. However, leaders who have developed a great rapport with their team won't have to do so anonymously if they have managed to create a supportive, friendly, and judgment-free working environment.

Great leaders need to understand that the total success of a team lies in how well they perform, whether they are high, moderate, or low performers. There is a limit to how well the best, i.e., the high performers of the team, will perform. Furthermore, high performers have a general drive to seek out new challenges and goals if they feel that they have achieved all that they can in their present capacity. Therefore, once leaders set a minimum standard everyone must meet, they can then focus on getting the moderate performers to improve themselves just enough to reach the next level.

At the same time, leaders should also focus on improving the performance of the supposed low performers, which include new people and people who are still looking to find their place. The keyword here is "supposed" because a leader should not be quick to label anyone as a low performer or underperformer until they can objectively admit that they have provided all the necessary performance feedback along with tools or methods to assist improvement, utilized the different coaching styles to connect with them, and provided constant positive encouragement.

Ultimately, the biggest benefit of coaching leadership is that it improves the overall knowledge of both the leader and the followers, increasing their confidence in themselves and trust in their abilities. This will enable them to work diligently to achieve their full potential, providing better employee satisfaction, and resulting in low company turnover.

On the other hand, coaching does come with its own share of challenges that keep it from becoming completely hassle-free. The biggest hurdle is leaders who are not well-versed in the art of coaching, for which they require empathy, patience, and understanding. Leaders who haven't had great coaches or mentors themselves and have largely focused on the bottom line rather than the big picture will find themselves seriously lacking in how to improve their employees' performance and offer them the right kind of guidance. They will also have their attention focused on the immediate goals of growth, targets, and performance metrics to prioritize employee development.

That's not to say that the onus is entirely on the leaders. It could also be due to employees who are complacent, unmotivated, or unwilling to be coached. They could have different opinions about what works for them, even if leaders know what they are talking about. This could be due to a lack of faith or trust in the leader or a lack of commitment and loyalty on the employees' part. Leaders must therefore learn how to tackle these challenges if they want to become great at coaching, not just for the team's sake but also for the long-term vision of the organization.

Encouragement, Not Praise

Take a hypothetical situation: A high performer suddenly starts delivering lower or even mediocre results. This is alarming because, up until now, they have been performing exceptionally well. Not only that, as the leader, you have been providing them with steady praise about how well they have been doing and also how others could use them as an example. So why have they started getting worse?

Coaching leadership requires that leaders recognize and appreciate their people's efforts. But how much appreciation is required? Should leaders restrain how much they appreciate their people? The answer is yes because too much praise can have a detrimental effect on the team members. Most leaders will immediately start praising their high performers in the hopes that they carry on their winning streak. The greater the praise, the higher the expectations. However, too much undue praise can create the perception among people that everything they do will be recognized. They become complacent and start resting on their laurels which has the opposite effect of what leaders expected.

Not only does this negatively impact the performance of the individual, but it also hurts the relationship between the person and the leader. High performers who were once adored and praised to the moon by their leaders will not take kindly to losing out on the praise and instead getting constructive or even harsh criticism. At the same time, leaders who have been unduly praising their high performers will be disappointed, not to mention upset or even furious that their praise has all been for nothing. This damages any trust and loyalty that the leader and follower have to each other and makes the whole experience transactional if nothing else.

For coaching leadership to work effectively, leaders need to keep their praise contingent upon results. Because leaders believe that praise can induce motivation from the get-go, they leave an environment that demands praise for no reason other than for showing up. It takes the notion of looking out for the employee's motivations too far instead of balancing it with the need for results and productivity.

This is where leaders need to understand that there is a difference between praising and encouraging someone. Praise depends upon the results an individual or team achieves, which is essential to keep them motivated only when they are successful. On the other hand, encouragement motivates people to achieve those results to earn that praise. Praise is supposed to be earned, while encouragement is essential for people to work hard and make the necessary efforts.

If leaders are unable to push their people towards improving or delivering results, then they need to reevaluate how they coach them. The most obvious sign of the success of coaching is that the employees are getting better and better as they move up from low to moderate to high performers. But in the absence of such progress, all leaders do is end up rewarding people for nothing.

Therefore, leaders should focus more on encouragement in their coaching by focusing on the potential their people have as well as their past achievements to help inspire them. This will enable leaders to foster better relationships with their people and bring their heads together to solve any lingering issues that are creating any hindrances to performance. At the same time, leaders also have to be honest with low or struggling performers about what is going wrong and let them know how they can amend it. This is how leaders can get much more effective at coaching as they collaborate with their people on figuring out how to solve their problems in order to make their goals attainable.

Until leaders see improvement and results, they should limit the amount of praise to a minimum. The encouragement should continue; however, leaders should avoid falling into the trap of trying to keep everyone happy. Oftentimes, leaders feel the need to be liked by their people, which makes them become sort of cheerleaders rather than coaches. The idea is that if leaders are always nice to their people with undue praise, they can build better relationships and a high-performing work environment. The most obvious signs of this are leaders pacing through the floor, giving high-fives for no reason, and offering compliments for no reason. Unfortunately, all this does is inflate the team's sense of self-importance, where they believe themselves to be the greatest thing since sliced bread. Moreover, it also doesn't do any favors to the people who are already struggling, as they see undue praise for high performers as something they aren't achieving and will not be able to achieve.

Instead, people who are genuinely concerned with their growth and performance will want their leaders to tell them what they are doing wrong as well as what they are doing right. They also want their leaders to tell them what more they can do to improve. People want their leaders to tell them their mistakes so that they can become the best versions of themselves and reach their full potential. This way, they can work harder and aspire towards justified praise for their results. That's not to say that leaders shouldn't praise people at all. If anything, leaders can praise people as much as they want, provided that they are meeting or going above expectations and delivering the expected results. Leaders should recognize the fine line between encouragement and praise and be sure to respect that boundary.

Your Feedback Counts

Please, leave a REVIEW
wherever you made your purchase.

Share your experience with
others help us grow our audience.

 Booksprout

For the opportunity to read advanced copies of our books, join our review team on BookSprout:

**https://booksprout.co/reviewer/team/
31264/panterax-book-review-team**

Conclusion

Your journey into Super Basic Leadership has only just begun.

The lessons highlighted in these pages have provided you with the roadmap of how you can become a great, successful, and meaningful leader, not just by understanding the kind of leader that you are but also the kind of leader you should be to your people. This includes staying calm and not letting your emotions get the better of you, being passionate about your goals and vision to inspire your people, setting an example by being ready to take on the same responsibilities that you expect of your followers, and being ready to have open, honest, and wholesome communication.

But while understanding these concepts has made you ask yourself several questions, don't forget that you also have the answers when it comes to becoming a leader that people can trust and who can leverage this trust to influence and achieve tremendous results.

All it takes is for you to be courageous and disciplined so that you recognize the challenges you have ahead of you and what efforts and sacrifices it will take to overcome them. At the same time, you must also be prepared for any and all consequences of your actions with patience, understanding, and a readiness to turn a misfortune in your favor.

The foundation for your leadership is based on trust, whether it is in yourself, your people, or the other way around. It requires you to be completely honest with yourself and accept any and all shortcomings with hope and optimism so that you can begin rectifying them. It requires you to be completely honest with your people when things go right and when they go wrong, and be prepared to celebrate their success or accept responsibility for the failure. And, of course, it also requires you to accept honesty when it comes from your people and followers, especially when they point out their criticisms of your decisions, actions, and leadership style. This is how building trust as a two-way street enriches both your lives and the lives of your people, thus making a mutually beneficial relationship.

It doesn't take much effort to build trust. Start from the little things such as taking care of their day-to-day problems, providing them with a calm, conducive, comfortable, and protected working environment to let them perform at their best, and keep encouraging and motivating them so that they feel appreciated. At the same time, listen when they tell you that they have a problem or if they feel apprehensive about the direction of your strategy. You should also be ready to offer a helping hand through suggestions and counsel when they come to you with problems outside of work so that they feel relaxed and assured that they have a friend in you.

This is important as leaders need to be not just sympathetic but also empathetic. Most leaders may appear to be all about business when it comes to the expectations of their people. But as we have reviewed in these pages, the easiest way to get the best out of your people is to understand where they are coming from and how you would feel if you were in their shoes. Your leadership relies a lot on your humanity, where you remember that your people are human beings. You can only be their leader in the truest sense when you have their best interests at heart. This is the only way you can be assured of their loyalty when the time comes for them to be there for you, not to mention earn their respect and admiration.

If you enjoyed reading *Super Basic Leadership*, then be sure to let us know what you thought about it in your review and how the lessons within have helped you better understand what it takes to be a leader. Additionally, we would be honored if you also picked up the first title in the *Super Basic* series. In *Super Basic Adulting* by Paul D. Pantera, readers will be able to gain more insights on developing and understanding how to be a functional adult. It helps readers, especially young readers, explore life, challenges, and milestones within adulthood and how they can navigate through some of the most tricky but rewarding situations.

Also, be sure to pick up a copy of the Pantheria Life Log Journal. Available in Black, Purple, and Navy editions, the Pantheria Life Log Journal offers a flexible combination of various helpful journaling methods, such as a Goal Setting and Personal Accountability Log, Planner, Note Keeper, Journal, and Health Log. These journals are ideal for people who are constantly on the move and prefer the bleeding out of raw information and feelings through the personal touch of a pen and paper rather than a cold and mechanical screen. It is also ideal for leaders who wish to keep their most intimate thoughts outside the electronic domain in order to avoid being compromised by competing entities, as well as for outdoor enthusiasts who spend a lot of their time in nature and don't wish to look at their screens for longer than they need to.

As a taste of what the Pantheria Media Collection has to offer you in terms of intuitive and memorable content, flip over to the next page to fill out your "The Story So Far" Declaration page. This will help you to recap your current life situation, vision, goals, and obstacles to overcome on your journey to becoming a great leader.

The Story So Far...

My Name is _____ Today is _____

I am _____ at _____
         (Title or Profession)   (Company, Team, Unit)

My Goal in life is _____
         (Big Goal or Vision you want before you die)

To get there I must (List some Major Milestones)

_____
_____
_____
_____

So Far I have (List Some Accomplishments)

_____
_____
_____
_____

For now, I must (List major obstacles or requirements)

_____
_____
_____

EVERYDAY, with EVERY PAGE,
I move closer to My Dream........

The Pantheria Life Log starts with you summarizing your life
and defining your future to guide your mind and activities.

PANTHERIA LIFE LOGS BY PANTERAX
Available on Amazon.com

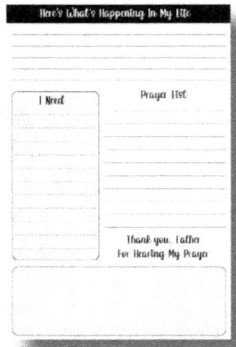

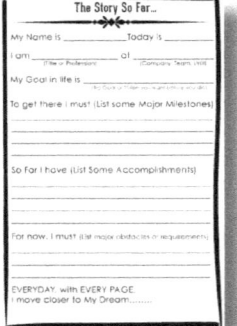

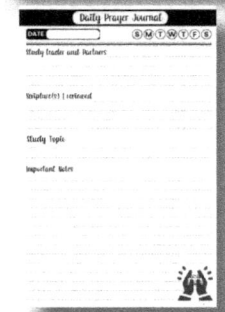

References

Auctor. (n.d.). WordSense Dictionary. https://www.wordsense.eu/auctor/

Baker, C. (2022, September 7). *Why is leadership important in business today?* Leaders. https://leaders.com/articles/leadership/why-is-leadership-important/

Bergeron, Z. (2015, December 9). *Great nan and trait theories vs. behavioural theories.* Prezi. https://prezi.com/qltyla8xweg6/great-man-and-trait-theories-vs-behavioural-theories/?frame=3d2dd37b9acc534e28f10380b594fd68367dd4b1

Bishop, C. (2018, November 14). *Influence, not authority, shows solid leadership.* Forbes. https://www.forbes.com/sites/forbeshumanresourcescouncil/2018/11/14/influence-not-authority-shows-solid-leadership/?sh=7c6b779b5eac

Bloom, N. A., Liang, J., Roberts, J., & Ying, Z. J. (2015). *Does working from home work? Evidence from a Chinese experiment.* The Quarterly Journal of Economics, (1), 165–218. https://doi.org/10.1093/qje/qju032

Center for Creative Leadership. (2022, September 4). *15 tips for effective communication in leadership.* https://www.ccl.org/articles/leading-effectively-articles/communication-1-idea-3-facts-5-tips/

Cherry, K. (2022, May 23). *The major leadership theories.* Verywell Mind. https://www.verywellmind.com/leadership-theories-2795323#toc-behavioral-theories

Cohen, H. (2012, July 17). *Fortune 500 CEOs don't get social media! [Research].* Heidi Cohen. https://heidicohen.com/fortune-500-ceos-dont-get-social-media-research/

Communities in School. (2017, February 7). *The importance of learning leadership at a young age.* https://cisjax.org/the-importance-of-learning-leadership-at-a-young-age/

Daskal, L. (n.d.). *How successful leaders build trust with their people.* Lolly Daskal. https://www.lollydaskal.com/leadership/how-successful-leaders-build-trust-with-their-people/

Dimock, M., & Gramlich, J. (2021, January 29). *How America changed during Trump's presidency.* Pew Research Center. https://www.pewresearch.org/2021/01/29/how-america-changed-during-donald-trumps-presidency/

Duckworth, A. (2016). *Grit: The power of passion and perseverance.* New York Scribner.

Eades, J. (2019, January 30). *How the best leaders put the needs of others before their own.* Inc.Africa. https://www.inc.com/john-eades/how-best-leaders-put-needs-of-others-before-their-own.html

Eastwood, B. (2019, January 24). *The 5 qualities all successful leaders have in common.* Northeastern University. https://www.northeastern.edu/graduate/blog/top-5-leadership-qualities/

Express Web Desk. (2019, September 7). *Chandrayaan-2: What Dr Abdul Kalam said on failure after ISRO's SLV-3 mission crashed.* The Indian Express. https://indianexpress.com/article/india/chandrayaan-2-dr-abdul-kalam-on-failure-after-isro-slv-3-mission-crash-5974097/

Fannin, K. (n.d.). *20 ways of developing leadership influence with trust.* Intelivate. https://www.intelivate.com/career-strategy/20-things-you-must-remember-about-trust#17-building-leadership-influence-start-with-building-trust-in-yourself

Geraci, J. (2016, December 27). *Embracing bad ideas to get to good ideas.* Harvard Business Review. https://hbr.org/2016/12/embracing-bad-ideas-to-get-to-good-ideas

Gordon, J [@JonGordon11]. (2016, April 25). *"A good coach can change a game. A great coach can change a life." -John Wooden* [Tweet]. Twitter. https://twitter.com/jongordon11/status/724396881003077634?lang=en

Guthrie-Jensen Consultants. (n.d.). *Top challenges that young business leaders face today.* Guthrie-Jensen. https://guthriejensen.com/blog/top-challenges-young-business-leaders-face/

IMD. (2022, August). *The 5 most common leadership styles & how to find yours.* https://www.imd.org/imd-reflections/reflection-page/leadership-styles/

Indeed Editorial Team. (2021, February 4). *What is the importance of leadership?* Indeed. https://www.indeed.com/career-advice/career-development/importance-of-leadership

Indeed Editorial Team. (2020, March 12). *What is coaching leadership? (And when to use this style).* Indeed. https://www.indeed.com/career-advice/career-development/coaching-leadership

Janse, B. (2019). *Great man theory.* toolshero. https://www.toolshero.com/leadership/great-man-theory/

Juhl, C. (2020, December 18). *Agreeing to disagree: Why leaders should encourage positive agitation.* GroupM. https://www.groupm.com/newsroom/agreeing-to-disagree-why-leaders-should-encourage-positive-agitation/

Kennedy, J. F. (n.d.). *Remarks prepared for delivery at the Trade Mart in Dallas, TX, November 22, 1963 [Undelivered].* The John F. Kennedy Presidential Library and Museum. https://www.jfklibrary.org/archives/other-resources/john-f-kennedy-speeches/dallas-tx-trade-mart-undelivered-19631122

Kim, K. (2002, May, 2). *The trust of the people in the leaders.* Laidlaw Scholars. https://laidlawscholars.network/posts/the-trust-of-the-people-in-the-leaders

Lalonde, J. (2022, February 12). *How leaders can navigate privacy with their team.* Biblical Leadership. https://www.biblicalleadership.com/blogs/how-leaders-can-navigate-privacy-with-their-team/

Lao-Tzu. (1993, October 15). *Tao Te Ching.* Hackett Publishing.

Leadership skills must be taught from a young age. (2019, May 11). UltraByte. https://www.ultrabyteit.com/leadership-skills/

Learnlight. (2018, January 29). *7 ways trust is a key international leadership quality.* https://www.learnlight.com/en/articles/trust-key-leadership-quality/

Lipschultz, B. (2021, March 8). *"Reddit Raider" favorite GameStop soars on latest Cohen push.* BNN Bloomberg. https://www.bnnbloomberg.ca/reddit-raider-favourite-gamestop-soars-after-latest-cohen-push-1.1573849

Mathur, A. (2021, December 13). *Scottie Pippen refusing to go into playoff game vs. Knicks shocked Steve Kerr: "He quit on us."* Sportscasting. https://www.sportscasting.com/scottie-pippen-refusing-playoff-game-knicks-shocked-steve-kerr/

McDermott, J. (2021, May 13). *The fortunes won – and lost – in the mind-boggling rise of r/WallStreetBets.* Esquire. https://www.esquire.com/lifestyle/money/a36395893/wallstreetbets-investment-fortunes-gamestop-inside-story/

Mcnish, J., & Silcoff, S. (2016). *Losing the signal: The spectacular rise and fall of Blackberry.* HarperCollins Publishers Ltd

Meehan, D. (2012, April 26). *Learning from stories of community leadership and change.* Leadership Learning Community. http:// leadershiplearning.org/blog/deborah-meehan/2012-04-26/ learning-stories-community-leadership-and-change

Mendenhall, M. E. (n.d.). *Leadership quotes.* The University of Tennessee Chattanooga. https://blog.utc.edu/mark-mendenhall/ leadership-resources/leadership-quotes/

Miech, C. (2022, March 31). *Spot the difference: Authority vs leadership.* TrackTime24. https://tracktime24.com/Blog/authority-vs-leadership

Milgram, S. (2010). *Obedience to authority.* Pinter & Martin. (Original work published 1974)

Morgan, J. (2020, May 7). *Research shows only 8% of leaders are great listeners and communicators.* Medium. https://medium.com/ jacob-morgan/research-shows-only-8-of-leaders-are-great-listeners-and-communicators-217343936ccd

Neale, P. (2020, June 24). *Building relationships and influencing people.* Forbes. https://www.forbes.com/sites/ forbescoachescouncil/2020/06/24/building-relationships-and-influencing-people/?sh=1990086058e6

Open Gate Consulting. (2021, January 26). *Self-discipline in leadership: Why is it so important?* https://www.opengateresources.com/self-discipline-in-leadership/

Piyu. (2019, June 12). *Difference between contingency and situational leadership.* DifferenceBetween.com. https://www. differencebetween.com/difference-between-contingency-and-situational-leadership/

Pratt, M. K. (n.d.). *Leadership.* TechTarget. https://www.techtarget.com/searchcio/definition/leadership

Repollé, N. (2018, December 4). *The 1st step in building great leaders: Knowing yourself.* Medium. https://medium.com/the-business-of-being-happy-and-healthy/the-1st-step-in-building-great-leaders-knowing-yourself-510e3e2403a4

Riegel, D. G. (2019, August 15). *8 ways leaders delegate successfully.* Harvard Business Review. https://hbr.org/2019/08/8-ways-leaders-delegate-successfully

Sostrin, J. (2018, April 17). *To be a great leader, you have to learn how to delegate well.* Harvard Business Review. https://hbr.org/2017/10/to-be-a-great-leader-you-have-to-learn-how-to-delegate-well

Surprising working from home productivity statistics. (2020). Apollo Technical. https://www.apollotechnical.com/working-from-home-productivity-statistics/

Talon, M. (2001, September 14). *Get IT done: IT pro's BlackBerry saved anguish during NYC attack.* TechRepublic. https://www.techrepublic.com/article/get-it-done-it-pros-blackberry-saved-anguish-during-nyc-attack/

The Dwight D. Eisenhower Presidential Library and Museum. (2022, September 20). *Quotes.* https://www.eisenhowerlibrary.gov/eisenhowers/quotes

The entrepreneur's guide to work/life balance. (2021, September 23). Keap. https://keap.com/business-success-blog/business-management/culture/work-life-balance

The role of strategist in a business organization. (n.d.) MBA Knowledge Base. https://www.mbaknol.com/management-concepts/the-role-of-strategist-in-a-business-organization/

3 leadership stories to help you be a better manager. (n.d.). Lighthouse. https://getlighthouse.com/blog/leadership-stories-help-better-manager/

21 community leaders who inspired us in 2021. (2022, June 21). Meta. https://about.fb.com/community-leader-spotlight-2021/

Vincze. (n.d.). *Understand yourself before anything else.* Thrive. https://thriveglobal.com/stories/understand-yourself-before-anything-else/

Walder, K. (n.d.). *The many facets of leadership roles.* Monster. https://www.monster.com/career-advice/article/getting-into-leadership-roles

Waters, S. (2021, October 15). *How using different types of authority affects leadership.* BetterUp. https://www.betterup.com/blog/types-of-authority

Weber, M., & Whimster, S. (2009). *The essential weber: A reader.* Routledge.

Welch, J., & Welch, S. (2007). *Winning.* Harper.

Youth leader demographics and statistics in the US. (2021, January 29). Zippia. https://www.zippia.com/youth-leader-jobs/demographics/

Image References

Amy Hirschi. (2019, March 6). *[Woman in teal t-shirt sitting beside woman in suit jacket]* [Image]. Unsplash. https://unsplash.com/photos/JaoVGh5aJ3E

Annie Spratt. (2018, March 22). *[Sitting people beside table inside room]* [Image]. Unsplash. https://unsplash.com/photos/hCb3lIB8L8E

Avi Richards. (2017, January 3). *Editing with a view* [Image] Unsplash. https://unsplash.com/photos/Z3ownETsdNQ

Baatcheet Films. (2022, January 12). *[Mahatma Gandhi statue]* [Image]. Unsplash. https://unsplash.com/photos/IQwRC4_AsGY

Colin Lloyd. (2021, March 28). *[Man in black police uniform holding usa flag]* [Image]. Unsplash. https://unsplash.com/photos/efrRLPZukCQ

Glenn Carstens-Peters. (2017, February 5). *[Person using MacBook Pro photo]* [Image]. Unsplash. https://unsplash.com/photos/npxXWgQ33ZQ

Headway. (2018, January 29). *[Black smartphone near person]* [Image]. Unsplash. https://unsplash.com/photos/5QgIuuBxKwM

Jason Goodman. (2019, March 15). *[Woman placing sticky notes on wall photo]* [Image]. Unsplash. https://unsplash.com/photos/Oalh2MojUuk

JESHOOTS.COM. (2018, April 16). *[Depth of field photography of man playing chess photo]* [Image]. Unsplash. https://unsplash.com/photos/fzOITuS1DIQ

Jo Szczepanska. (2018, November 19). *[Sticky notes on corkboard photo]* [Image]. Unsplash. https://unsplash.com/photos/5aiRb5f464A

Kevin Bhagat. (2017, August 17). *Workhard Anywhere* [Image]. Unsplash. https://unsplash.com/photos/zNRITe8NPqY

krakenimages. (2020, September 23). *Group of business workers standing with hands together doing symbol at the office* [Image]. Unsplash. https://unsplash.com/photos/Y5bvRlcCx8k

Miguel Bruna. (2018, January 6). *2018 he we come!* [Image]. Unsplash. https://unsplash.com/photos/TzVN0xQhWaQ

Miguel Henriques. (2018, December 11). *[Man speaking in front of crowd photo]* [Image]. Unsplash. https://unsplash.com/photos/RfiBK6Y_upQ

Priscilla Du Preez. (2017, April 6). *[People laughing and talking outside during daytime]* [Image]. Unsplash. https://unsplash.com/photos/nF8xhLMmg0c

Riccardo Annandale. (2016, September 23). *[Man holding incandescent bulb]* [Image]. Unsplash. https://unsplash.com/photos/7e2pe9wjL9M

Shelagh Murphy. (2019, January 16). *[Person raising right hand photo]* [Image]. Unsplash. https://unsplash.com/photos/xy1oUOqobFA

Visit Us Online

https://pantheria.store

a Find our Books on Amazon

▶ Pantheria

📷 @Pantheria.lofi

f @Pantheria.lofi

www.ingramcontent.com/pod-product-compliance
Lightning Source LLC
Chambersburg PA
CBHW071329120626
46546CB00002B/499